CYCLING

in and around

LONDON

Compiled by the North London, South-West London,
West Kent and West London District Associations
of the Cyclists' Touring Club

Edited by John Franklin

John Bartholomew & Son Limited

MAP LEGEND

Route 1

▬▬ Cycle route

— Circular route

■ ■ ■ Sections of routes to be walked

■ 180 Place of interest with text reference

▲ Youth hostel

→ One-way street

🔟 Starting place for Out-of-London route

a b Cycling information in text

Routes 2-5

▬ Cycle route

— Other roads

▬ ▬ ▬ Sections of routes to be walked

• • • • • Unmetalled track

■ P Place of interest with text reference

▲ Youth hostel

→ One-way street

╫ Traffic signals along routes (excluding pelicans)

⬦ Roundabout

rupp Road used as a public path

⑲ Connecting Out-of-London route

a b Cycling information in text

Routes 6-37

— Minor road

▬ Classified road

· · · · · · Unmetalled track

- — - Alternative route

■ Town, village or place of interest along route

□ Town, village or place of interest off route

▲ Youth hostel along route

△ Youth hostel off route

⁺⁺⁺•⁺ Railway with station

→ One-way street

┤ Traffic signals (excluding pelicans) ⎤ Suburban maps only

⬦ Roundabout ⎦

▬ Towpath ⎤ Routes 23

▬ Bridge ⎬ and 24

▬ Lock ⎦ only

★ 20a Route break with continuation map number

Shepperton Route break and change of

✪ 15c map scale with continuation map number

REIGATE ■ Destination

Radlett Place mentioned in text

Ealing Other place

⑧ Connecting route

a b Cycling information in text

First published in Great Britain 1981 by
John Bartholomew and Son Limited,
© **Cyclists' Touring Club**

ISBN: 0 7028 8051 5

*British Library Cataloguing in Publication
Data*

The Bartholomew/CTC guide to cycling in
and around London
  1. Cycling — London
  I. Franklin, John
  796.6'09421 GV1052.G727L/

CYCLING IN AND AROUND LONDON

CONTENTS

INTRODUCTION

Cycling is a great way of travelling around London. The bicycle is an ideal form of transport for the commuter or shopper as it is cheaper, more convenient, more reliable and usually quicker than public transport or motoring. The regular exercise cycling provides is very healthy too. Cycling is also an excellent way of seeing London and its surrounding countryside offering the tourist greater accessibility than a car, train or bus and a greater range than walking. Indeed, by combining any of these aspects of cycling even the most mundane journeys can be a pleasure.

It is understandable, however, that many people view the prospect of cycling in London with some trepidation. Many streets are narrow and heavily congested and elsewhere traffic usually travels much faster than it does in most other towns and cities; although often only from one traffic jam to the next. Furthermore, many roads are badly designed from a cyclist's point of view and suffer from the noise and pollution of motor traffic. In practice, cycling in London is not as hazardous as at first seems and if you follow the advice given later in this book it can actually be enjoyable. Learning the necessary skills is well worth the little effort involved, for cycling in London has many benefits as an increasing number of people are discovering.

This book aims to encourage an interest in cycling both for utility and pleasure by offering a selection of routes, most of which are suitable in whole or part for the commuter or cycle-tourist. It is not intended as a comprehensive guide to all routes which are suitable, nor are the routes shown necessarily ideal throughout their length. Rather this is an attempt to define a number of routes which are both useful and interesting and which avoid, as far as they are able, major traffic blackspots. Advice on choosing further routes to suit individual requirements is given in the section on 'Cycling in traffic'.

1. CYCLING IN TRAFFIC

Safe cycling in London is a combination of two factors: adopting an appropriate riding technique and choosing suitable routes.

Riding technique

Cycling in London is markedly different from riding in quieter environments and therefore requires a different technique. The approach should be basically defensive. One reason why drivers and pedestrians give less consideration to cyclists than they should is that they too have many more problems to contend with than in smaller towns or the countryside. Cyclists have a right to be on the road and should not be afraid to exert that right whenever it is safe to do so but try not to be too aggressive or assume an aura of superiority over others for that will surely be reflected in how those people react to other cyclists.

You are at your safest if you are able to keep up with traffic and to move as part of it, for drivers are then more likely to respect your presence and not take risks just to overtake you. On many London roads, where traffic moves in fits and starts, keeping up is not too difficult for people who are reasonably fit, but it is helpful to have a cycle equipped with a wide range of gears and adjusted correctly to suit the rider. In this way machine and rider respond as one. In congested traffic the use of low gears will enable you to maintain momentum by pedalling fast and also to accelerate rapidly when necessary. Change down in gear before you stop and on approaching junctions just in case you need to stop, so that you can restart with reasonable ease. In this way cyclists can often accelerate from a standstill faster than cars for the first few yards and this is valuable in reducing the chances of being overtaken on a junction. As you move away, change up again in order to maintain your advantage for as long as possible, over following traffic, but it is not advisable to engage too high a gear unless the road ahead is clear for some appreciable distance.

Road positioning is an important aspect of safe cycling. Contrary to the opinion of some, cyclists are not obliged to keep close to the kerb and should not always do so. Ride at least an outstretched arm's distance away so that you can avoid drains, potholes and the debris which invariably ends up in this part of the road. This will leave a 'safe area' into which to retreat should you be overtaken dangerously. Approaching junctions, road works, and width restrictions, occupy the left hand traffic lane in such a way as to prevent yourself being overtaken in that lane. This is particularly important at the approach to roundabouts and traffic signals for if you are first in the queue it helps to prevent the dangerous practice of a driver turning left in front of a cyclist, a frequent cause of cycle accidents.

When there are long queues leading to a junction it is understandable that cyclists will not wish to wait at the back if there is space for them to pass. However, pass down the outside of the queue only when all traffic in front is stationary. Look out for opening doors and try to get back to a centre-of-lane position before the traffic starts moving again. At least catch the eye of the driver behind to make sure that he knows you are there. Even if you are able to get to the front of the queue while other traffic waits, it is wise not to pass the side of the front vehicle as that driver or rider will be concentrating most on the traffic conditions at the junction and might easily not see a cyclist come alongside.

On wanting to turn right, signal clearly well in advance of the junction and move towards the centre of the road in good time. In congested traffic change position one lane at a time. Again occupy the centre of the lane for right turning traffic until you are at the junction itself when you should seek a traffic island or another turning vehicle for protection if you have to wait.

Whenever manoeuvring or turning it is essential to be definite and decisive about your intentions for well-signalled and executed manoeuvres are much more likely to be respected by motorists than hesitant ones. Most drivers in London are familiar with the roads they are using and do not give too much consideration to strangers who are unsure as to which route to take. Keep alert and always try to anticipate the stupid things that other road users sometimes do. A common cause of accidents to cyclists is the careless opening of offside car doors, so try to leave sufficient clearance when overtaking parked cars, particularly those with occupants. Another common cause of accidents is when a driver overtakes a cyclist and then pulls in sharply to stop or turn left. Glance over your shoulder when approaching junctions and try not to signal left turns too early for this sometimes encourages motorists also wishing to turn left to overtake on the junction.

An increasing problem in London, as elsewhere, is the deteriorating condition of many road surfaces due to potholes, badly reinstated trenches, etc. Councils have a legal obligation to keep the roads in a safe condition so report any bad examples which you meet and insist that action be taken. However, realistically this will remain a problem for a long time and it is therefore necessary to be alert for the presence of defects when riding and to be prepared to take counter-action. If possible, position yourself in good time to avoid holes and bumps. However, your ability to do this safely will depend upon following traffic of which you should always be aware. If such surface defects are unavoidable, steer a straight course and take your weight off the saddle by standing on the pedals. This will minimize discomfort to yourself and reduce the possibility of damage to your cycle. However, should your cycle be damaged or you suffer any injury, do not be afraid to seek financial compensation from the local council, quoting the location and time of the incident.

Although it is preferrable to ride at a speed compatible with traffic, a cyclist must appreciate that generally his brakes will operate less quickly than those of other vehicles, especially if it is wet. You should therefore always ride with hands on the brake levers when in traffic in order to be able to reduce speed at the slightest indication of trouble ahead. Be particularly careful in streets crowded with pedestrians, who may not hear a cycle approach, and near schools and playgrounds where children may suddenly run out into the road. A horn can sometimes be useful if there is little traffic around, but otherwise it is much more effective and colourful to shout and have your hands ready for applying the brakes.

If riding after dark, make sure that your lights are in good working order and try to wear light-coloured clothes. If using dynamo lighting, be particularly careful making right turns as your lights will go out if you have to stop.

Choosing routes

A good map is the key to selecting routes and it should show the minor road network in detail over the whole of the area across which you wish to travel. In central London Bartholomew's *Everyone's London* street plan is ideal and has the added advantage of depicting one-way streets. For the suburbs and other urban areas the Ordnance Survey 1:50,000 series is best while in country areas Bartholomew's 1:100,000 series is also suitable. Street atlases are less suitable for route planning as each page covers too limited an area but they can be useful for route following.

Try to work out all the possible ways in which your journey could be made in a reasonably direct and convenient manner. If it is intended to make the journey regularly, say for commuting, the only real way to find out which is the best route is to try them all. For what looks best - or worst - on paper is not necessarily always so in practice. For instance, although it is generally safer to use minor roads rather than main ones, a free-flowing dual carriageway can be much safer than narrow residential streets lined with parked cars or where a cyclist frequently has to give way to crossing traffic. Information such as this cannot be gleaned from a map. Remember too that any route is only as safe as its most dangerous point.

If a journey is a 'one-off' or made only infrequently, there are a number of guidelines which will give a good chance of finding the best route to use. Probably the biggest problems for cyclists to overcome are large roundabouts and gyratory systems. Avoid these if you possibly can. Roads used extensively by heavy goods vehicles also present difficulties, particularly where there is little room for overtaking. The trunk roads carry most of this traffic and these are identified by a (T) suffix on maps. Note, however, that the trunk road designation is not used in central London. Try to avoid these roads too. Conversely roads which are paralleled by motorways are usually relatively free of heavy traffic.

When there is a choice, choose minor roads in preference to 'B' roads and 'B' roads as against 'A' roads. In town, the minor roads coloured yellow on OS maps will usually be the easiest to follow but those which are white may also be convenient. The extent to which a cyclist will wish to follow a complex route along minor roads in order to avoid busy roads will depend very much upon his journey purpose. It has already been indicated that minor roads are not necessarily safer

than main ones. Commuters and other cyclists wishing to complete their journey in as short a time as possible will often be happier following a reasonably direct route, but using minor roads where possible. On the other hand, the cycle-tourist with time to spare will probably find a less direct route more interesting as this will give a much better appreciation of the area through which he or she is passing than can be obtained from the usual through routes.

In country areas the roads coloured yellow on OS or Bartholomew's maps are invariably the best to use as they have more character as well as being quieter. In most parts of the country cyclists can quite easily keep clear of classified roads for most of the time. Beyond the area covered by this book *CTC Route Guide to Cycling in Britain and Ireland* details a network of such routes throughout the country.

Sometimes minor road routes can be linked together by using short stretches of footpath or bridleway. Take care at these places, give way to pedestrians and dismount if there are 'No Cycling' signs. If you consider that such a link could usefully be upgraded to a cycle path, tell the local authority.

In many parts of London new cycle routes and other special cycle 'facilities' are being introduced. Often these will provide safer and convenient routes for cyclists but this is not always the case. In particular, a number of arterial roads in outer London have cycle tracks alongside. These have been clearly proven, over many years, to be much less safe for cyclists than the main carriageway, even when they are not obstructed by parked cars or strewn with broken glass and other debris. It is usually best to avoid them.

2. INTRODUCTION TO THE ROUTES

The routes

All routes in this book are designed to show suitable ways for cyclists to ride between places of interest in and around London but their character-istics and presentation vary considerably from one to another.

Some routes are linear, some are circular and others take the form of a network, leaving the rider to choose the one most suitable for his or her purpose. The routes cover a wide range of distances. Some very interesting rides of only a few miles can be selected from the networks of routes while the more ambitious cyclist can ride as far as the 71 miles to Oxford or even attempt the 150 miles of the London grand orbital route in one go! Likewise there is a choice of terrain. As the London Basin is predominantly flat, so are the majority of the routes and, indeed, the two towpath routes are almost literally so. But the routes to the Northern Heights, Crystal Palace and the North Downs climb to higher ground, rewarding the extra effort with fine views as well as much of interest.

London is one of the most fascinating cities in the world to explore but it can also be a joy to escape to the peace of the surrounding countryside. To cater for the diverse needs of London cyclists, residents and visitors alike, some routes are wholly urban, some wholly in the countryside - with access by train or car - and some traverse both types of environment. Many of the urban routes can be of value to both the town commuter and leisure rider and some of the longer journeys, notably those to Heathrow and Gatwick Airports, also have a utilitarian function as well as being interesting in their own right.

The routes have not been chosen to a common standard but vary according to location in order to provide the best cycling environment among the choice of routes available. Generally the busier main roads are avoided but some of the out-of-London routes do use 'A' roads through the suburbs where minor roads could be tedious given the desire to reach the countryside in a reasonable time. In some cases the suburban excursions provide alternatives for those with more time to spare. Other routes make use of main roads where there is no practical alternative or in order to reach places of interest which are accessible in no other way.

Bridleways and RUPPs (roads used as public paths) are included in a few routes but unless these are surfaced for all-weather cycling road alternatives are also shown. Short lengths of footpath, for which it is necessary to dismount, are also included where they form useful links.

Several out-of-London routes terminate at, or pass close by places with youth hostels. Such accommodation is very popular with cyclists and could be used to enable some of the longer rides to be undertaken as weekend trips. Other accommodation - camping, bed and breakfast, hotels - can also usually be found.

Cross-referencing between routes allows these to be combined to increase the permutations of different rides possible. The towpath and orbital routes are particularly useful for creating circular trips by linking together radial routes. The starting points of all the out-of-London routes are shown on the central London maps (Route 1).

One section of this book gives details of specific rail-assisted routes but trains - or a car - could also be used in conjunction with other routes in order to reduce distance or time spent passing through the suburbs.

The maps

All the routes are accompanied by maps but it is intended that these be used in conjunction with larger scale commercial maps to which reference is made. The maps are numbered to correspond with routes directly: for instance Map 1 accompanies Route 1, Map 10 accompanies Route 10, etc. In almost all cases the maps are divided into two or more sections and these are distinguished by suffices: e.g. Maps 4a, 4b, 4c.

The information given on the maps varies with the location, the underlying theme being that more detail is desirable towards the centre of London where the road system is more complex. The central London maps (Route 1) show the recommended routes against a background of all roads. The surburban excursions (Routes 2 to 5) show a background of major roads sufficient to relate the routes to a more detailed map. The out-of-London routes (Routes 6 to 22) are accompanied by two types of map: large scale line maps for the suburban sections of the routes which show the crossing points of all principal roads (roads shown in yellow on OS maps as well as classified roads) and smaller scale line maps for the country sections which show only the crossing points of classified roads. Similar scales are generally used for maps of the same type except the country sections of the out-of-London routes where one of two significantly different scales is used depending upon the length of the routes. It is important, therefore, always to check the scale bar shown on each map section.

Except for Route 1, road names are shown only along the routes themselves and within the suburban area. Near complex junctions some omission of names has been unavoidable and it is here that cross-reference to commercial maps can be particularly useful. Off the routes, main roads are identified only by their 'A' or 'B' numbers, which will usually be sufficient for comparison with other maps. On country area maps only classified roads are specifically labelled; towns and villages will act as further reference points.

The symbols used on maps varies to some extent between map types according to the differing detail

depicted. Reference should be made to the appropriate map key on pages 10 and 11.

Important, too, is the need to look at the north mark on each map section as the radial nature of many routes and the twisting course of some makes it necessary for successive maps and sections sometimes to vary in orientation. Usually the variation between the sections of one map is less than 30° but in the case of the Grand Union Canal towpath (Route 23), the change is more than 90°.

To maintain a north direction towards the top of each map, out-of-London maps north of the Thames read upwards leaving central London whereas maps south of the Thames read downwards.

Tourist information

Places of interest along or near the routes are marked either with numbers, letters or bold type and brief details are given in the accompanying text. Where possible, mention is made of places which are regularly open to the public and opening times are given. These details are, however, subject to alteration, particularly in winter months, and should be checked in advance if you wish to avoid disappointment.

Properties under the care of the National Trust or the Department of the Environment are indicated NT and DoE respectively.

Following the routes

Assistance from commercial maps is essential for easy following of the routes in this book. Check your route before you set out in order to clarify any uncertainties. On the road, consult maps only after you have pulled in out of the way, never while you are actually riding.

To aid route following, the text contains notes on particular points for attention and the location of these are marked on the maps with lower case italic letters. On the suburban maps the presence of traffic signals and roundabouts is shown as a navigation aid, but pedestrian ('Pelican') crossing signals have not been included.

Central London in particular is a labyrinth of one-way streets, banned turns, road closures and other restrictions and it has not been possible to indicate all of these. Also new restrictions are frequently being introduced. Sometimes it has been necessary to ignore the presence of these in the designation of the routes in order to maintain continuity. Care should therefore be exercised when following the routes as it may continue past a 'No Through Road' or 'No Entry' sign. This does not imply that cyclists may, or should, ride past these restrictions but where there is no specific cycle exemption the best solution is to dismount and walk. In almost all cases the distance to be walked will be short. In many cases where one-way streets are marked on the maps, a counter-flow route is also shown.

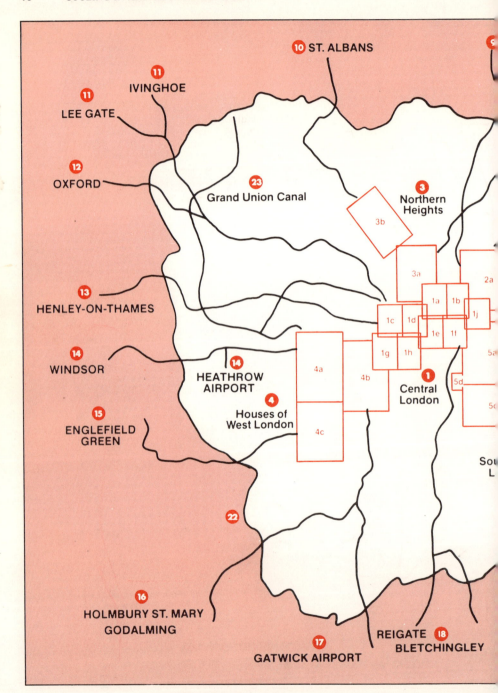

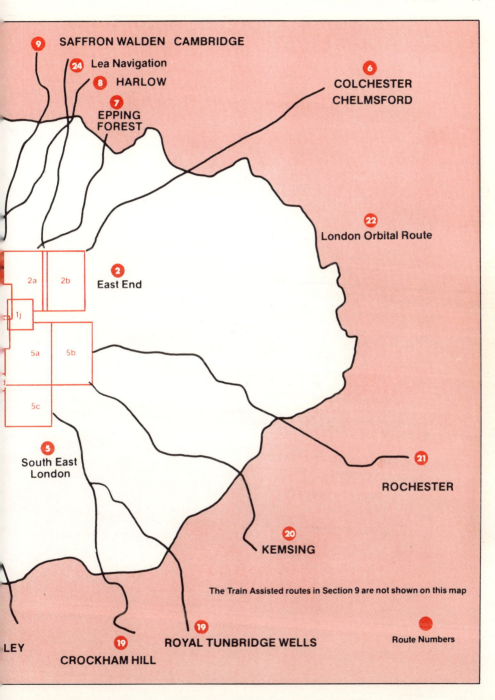

9 SAFFRON WALDEN CAMBRIDGE

24 Lea Navigation

8 HARLOW

7 EPPING FOREST

6 COLCHESTER CHELMSFORD

22 London Orbital Route

2a 2b

2 East End

1j

5a 5b

5c

5 South East London

21 ROCHESTER

20 KEMSING

The Train Assisted routes in Section 9 are not shown on this map

19 ROYAL TUNBRIDGE WELLS

19 CROCKHAM HILL

LEY

Route Numbers

3. CENTRAL LONDON

Almost every part of Central London is busy with traffic and pedestrians, but the routes shown avoid the busiest parts as far as possible and many are along very quiet back streets.

All the principal 'sights' of London are covered plus a large number of interesting minor sights which are unknown to most residents and visitors.

Although the network of routes permits countless permutations of journeys to suit the tourist or commuter, the sights are numbered in a such a way as to form a series of distinct linear sub-routes for exploring the area:

1- 17: North Kensington — Olympia — Hammersmith
18- 39: Little Venice — Kensington Palace — Earl's Court — Fulham — Walham Green
40- 65: Paddington — Hyde Park — Kensington — Victoria — Buckingham Palace — Westminster
66- 90: Westminster — Trafalgar Square — Covent Garden — British Museum — Lincoln's Inn
91-116: Chancery Lane — St Paul's — Tower of London — Spitalfields
117-142: Spitalfields — Barbican — St Pancras — Regent's Park
143-156: Baker Street — Wallace Collection — Royal Academy
157-177: Chelsea/Kensington — Tate Gallery — Westminster
178-203: Westminster — Waterloo — London Bridge
204-207: London Bridge — Shad Thames
208-225: St John's Wood — Regent's Park — London Telecom Tower — Lincoln's Inn — Covent Garden

226-242: Senate House — Leicester Square — Piccadilly — Mayfair
243-247: Regent Street — Langham Place — Marylebone
248-266: Camden Town — King's Cross — Finsbury — Islington
267-277: City — Bethnal Green

Additionally a circular route is depicted on the maps by a solid line for those wishing to see a representative selection of what London has to offer in a limited time. Ridden non-stop this route would take about two hours and most of the places passed could be visited within a day. Because of the numerous one-way roads, this route is best cycled in a general anti-clockwise direction.

The places of interest noted are the main features on the routes but the observant cyclist will see a great deal more. Look for torch snuffers, relics of the pre-street lighting days, old-fashioned shops, ornate ironwork and other points of detail. Look for the tell-tale signs of the growth of London from the Roman remains in the City, expanding in the 17th century to Spitalfields and Covent Garden, in the 18th century to Mayfair and still more in the 19th century to cover the whole of the central area. Industry and transport have also left their marks, particularly along the river, canals and railway.

Most things can be bought in London. The main shopping areas are Oxford Street, Regent Street, Bond Street, Knightsbridge and Kensington High Street and there are also thriving street markets at Petticoat Lane, Portobello Road, Chapel Market, Berwick Street, Exmouth Street and Lower Marsh. Some areas specialize: books on Charing Cross Road, electronics on Tottenham Court Road.

Route 1
THE SIGHTS OF CENTRAL LONDON

Bartholomew: *Everyone's London*

a Three steps.

b Walk through paths between flats.

c Dismount to use footbridge.

d Going south, walk along pavement on south side of Marylebone Road between Enford Street and Wyndham Street.

e Holland Park closes at dusk.

f There is foot access to the Hallfield Estate off Inverness Terrace.

g Cycling is allowed in Hyde Park along the paths and roads shown. The park closes from midnight to 0500hrs.

h A short path links Albion Gate with The Ring.

j The route between Rotten Row and The Carriage Road crosses the sandy horse ride   Take care.

k Cycling is permitted along the closed road past the Albert Memorial. Take care, however, at the junctions at either end of this road as the traffic signals take no account of the cycle route.

l Dismount to use short footpath.

m Walk through pedestrian gate.

n Two steps in gateway link Ennismore Street and Rutland Street.

p The route westward from Holland Park Avenue to Addison Gardens is signed as a cycle route to Shepherd's Bush and Hammersmith and includes use of a contra-flow cycle lane.

q A cycle crossing of Park Lane is proposed at Stanhope Gate. Until this is introduced, dismount to use the pedestrian subways beneath this dangerous road.

r Flight of steps. The alternative route is via Marlborough Road by St James's Palace.

s To turn right from Waterloo Station, either turn left and U-turn or dismount and walk.

t A cycle path through Bishop's Park links Stevenage Road and Bishop's Avenue with Putney Bridge Approach. To connect with roads east of Putney Bridge, dismount to use the pedestrian tunnel beneath the bridge.

u A footpath links King's Road with the corner of Carlyle Square

v Albert Bridge is one-way during peak hours. Dismounting is necessary to reach Cheyne Walk.

w Steps.

x Dismounting necessary.

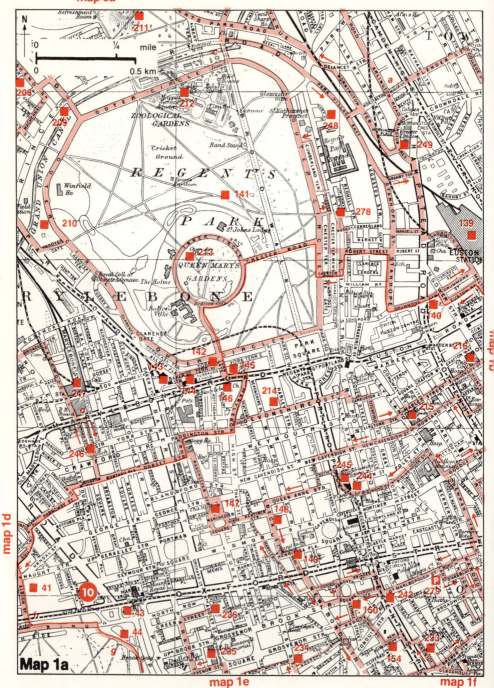

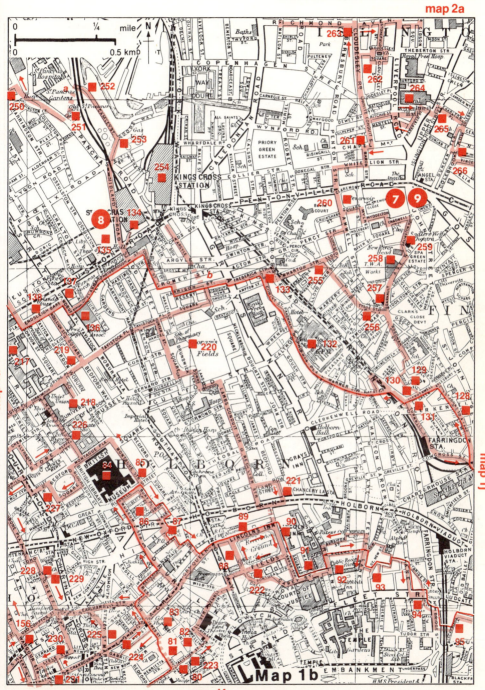

map 2a

map 1j

map 1f

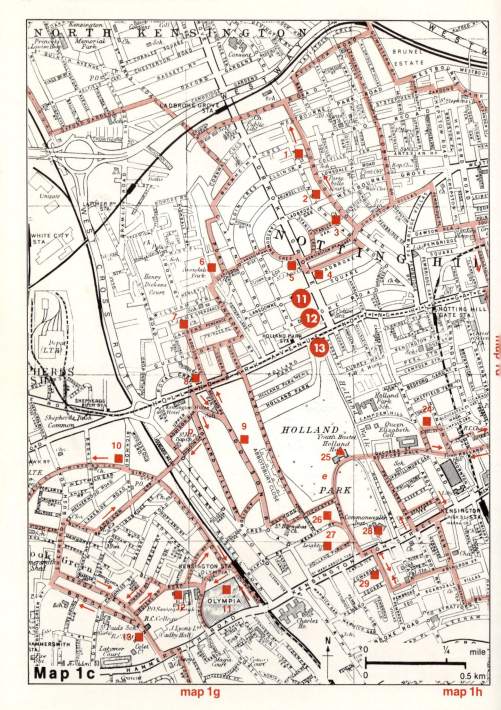

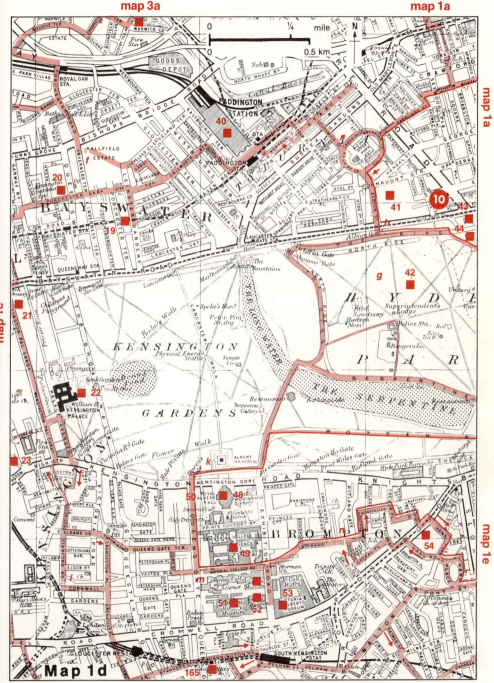

map 1a

map 1e

Map 1d

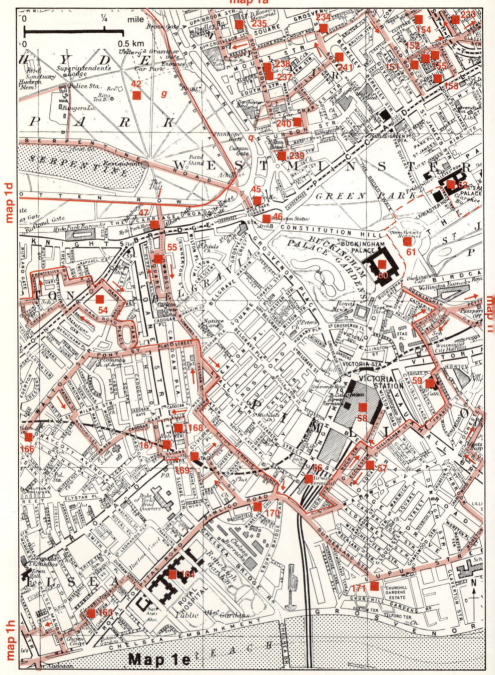

map 1a

map 1d

map 1i

map 1h

Map 1e

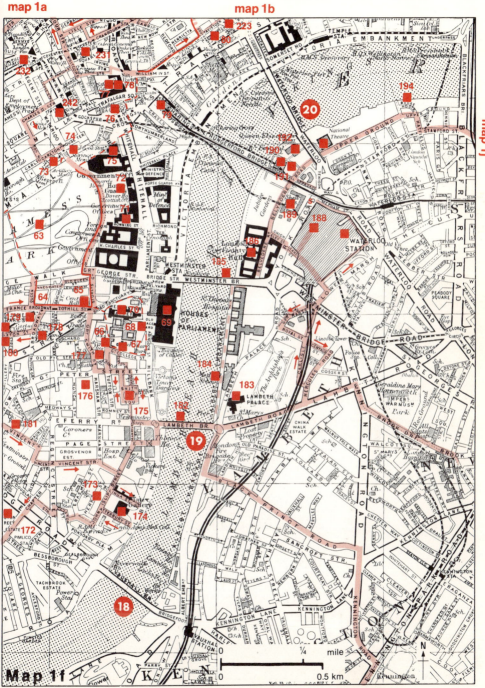

map 1a

map 1b

map 1j

map 5a

Map 1f

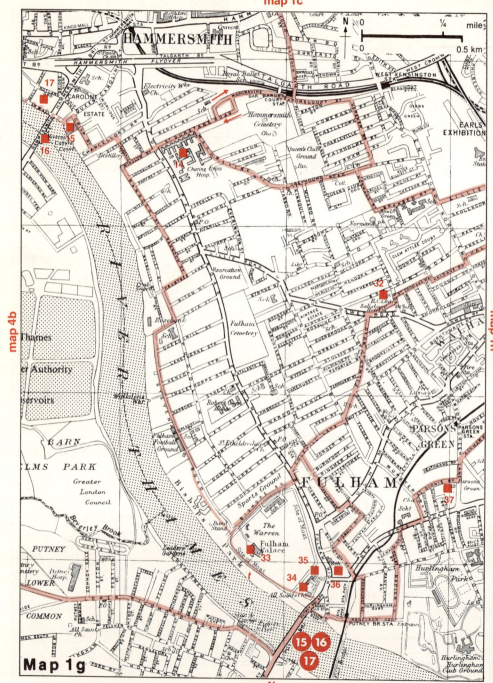

map 1c

HAMMERSMITH

map 4b

map 1h

Map 1g

map 4b

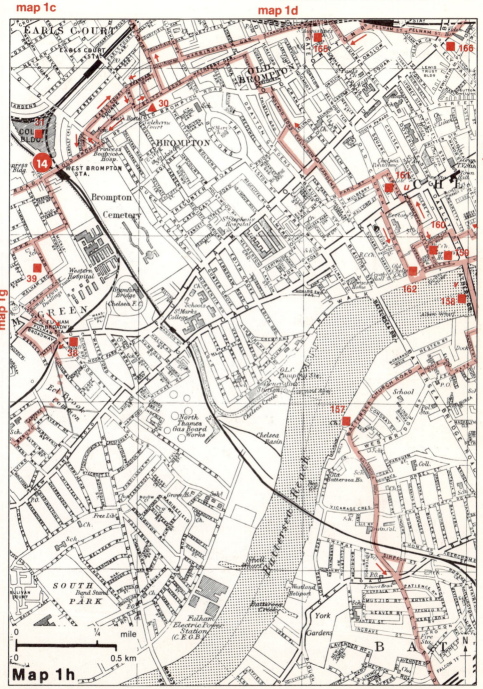

map 1c

map 1d

map 1e

map 1g

Map 1h

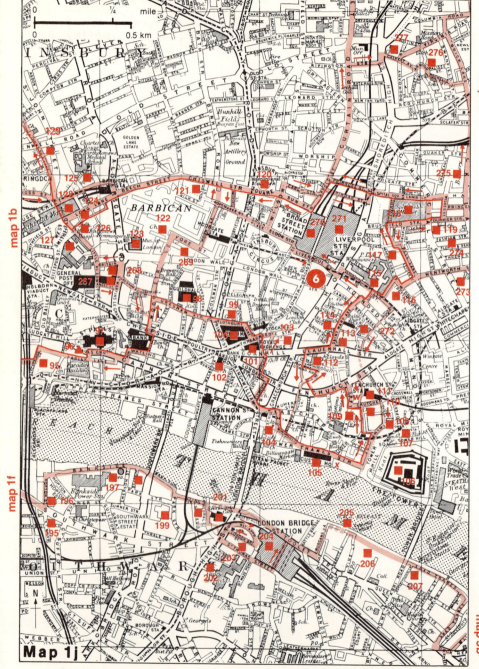

Map 1j

1 Electric Cinema: an early picture house now revived.

2 Portobello Road: antique shops and a Saturday street market.

3 St Peter's Church and Stanley Park Gardens: 1850, well-composed stucco development using newly discovered cement facing.

4 Ladbroke Square Gdns: largest private gardens in Kensington, 1840-50.

5 St John's Church: 1845, on site of Notting Hill farm. 1837-41 site of Hippodrome racecourse.

6 The Kiln: rebuilt 1879 following redevelopment of slum area. Relic of potteries established from 1820s.

7 St James's Church: 1844, 12thC Gothic style to match estate.

8 Royal Crescent: 1846, good composition.

9 No. 8 Addison Road: unusual tile design, 1906.

10 London and South Western Railway: sign remains on bridge. Offices built since railway closed in 1914.

11 Olympia Exhibition Halls: 1866-1930, ugly concrete.

12 National Savings Bank: 1903 red brick Queen Anne Style.

13 St Joseph's Almshouses: 1851.

14 Charing Cross Hospital: moved here 1973, on site with 1881 Fulham workhouse hospital. Whole area developed late 19thC on former market gardens.

15 Riverside Theatre: formerly television studios, now a small theatre offering plays, concerts, poetry, etc.

16 Hammersmith Bridge. by Bazalgette, 1887, on piers of original 1827 bridge.

17 Lower Mall: riverside houses, 17thC to early 19thC.

18 Little Venice: junction of Grand Junction and Regent's canals. Old tollhouse, water bus to the zoo in the summer.

19 23-24 Leinster Gardens: sham fronts hiding Circle Line underground.

20 Queensway: 1837, Whiteleys store, 1912, was earliest London departmental store, founded 1862.

21 Kensington Palace Gardens: 1840, many embassies, Private road but cycles allowed.

22 Kensington Palace: 1689, Wren. Still occupied by Royalty. State apartments open 1000-1800 (Sun from 1400, winter to 1600). Kensington Gardens open till dusk.

23 St Mary Abbots: rebuilt by G Scott 1872. 278ft spire, the tallest in London. Quality shopping on Kensington High Street.

24 Observatory Gardens: site of world's largest telescope 1831. Housing built 1880s;

25 Holland Park: Remains of 200 acres bought by Baron Holland 1748. 1605 house bombed 1940 but part restored for YHA. Peacocks in woods.

26 Tower House: by William Burgess in style of his restored castle at Castell Coch, near Cardiff.

27 Leighton House Art Gallery: 1866. Victorian Art. Open 1100-1700, not Suns. Free.

28 Commonwealth Institute: 1962. Exhibitions, films, etc. Open 1000-1730, 1430-1900 Suns. Free.

29 Edwardes Square: 1813. Gardens protected from building by Act of Parliament.

30 Earl's Court Youth Hostel: Bolton Gdns.

31 Earl's Court Exhibition Hall: largest reinforced concrete building when opened in 1937.

32 St Thomas's: 1849, by Pugin. One of his many Catholic Churches.

33 Fulham Palace: 1510 country home of Bishops of London. Moat — the largest in the country — filled in 1921 and now public gardens. Pretty entrance lodge. *c.*1810.

34 Fulham Church Tower: *c.*1440 with 15thC glass.

35 No. 6 Church Gate: *c.*1800, fire insurance mark.

36 Fulham Pottery: 17thC, kiln, 18thC. Shop sells pots.

37 St Dionis: 1884, the pulpit and altar are from a Wren City church. Houses *c.*1840.

38 Fulham Town Hall: 1890, classical.
39 Former horse bus garage and stables: 1903.
40 Paddington Station: 1854. Ornate offices by Brunel on Platform 1.
41 Edgware and Bayswater Roads: Roman Watling Street and Ad Pontem. 1827-61 development by Bishop of London of Tyburn estate to Praed Street.
42 Hyde Park: belonged to the Abbey of Westminster. Henry VIII converted it to a deer park, the Stuarts to horse racing. Queen Anne made improvements and Queen Caroline dammed the Westbourne river to form the Serpentine, 1637 .
43 Marble Arch: built by Nash in 1828 as entrance to Buckingham Palace. Moved to present site 1851. Oxford Street shops start there.
44 Speakers' Corner: mainly at weekends and during summer.
45 Apsley House: Duke of Wellington's town residence, now museum. 1778 by Robert Adam. Contains Duke's personal relics and Valasquez paintings. Open Tu,Thu,Sat 1000-1800, Sun 1430-1800. Free.
46 Constitution Arch, Hyde Park Corner: 1825 Decimus Burton design, built 1846. Ionic columns. Charity placed on top 1912. Sunday morning traffic may be light enough to cycle straight across from Hyde Park, but otherwise walk through subways.
47 Albert Gate: 1845, Built over the Westbourne river.
48 Royal Albert Hall: 1871 and venue for concerts, etc. Faces Albert Memorial, also 1871, by Gilbert Scott. South Kensington 'education area' purchased from proceeds of 1851 Great Exhibition on site of market gardens.
49 Imperial College of Science & Technology: 1906. 280ft Queens Tower remains from 1887 Imperial Institute.
50 Science Museum: 1928, free. Open Mon-Fri 1000-1800. Sat and Sun 1430-1800.
51 Natural History Museum: Waterhouse 1881, free. Open as Science Museum.

52 Geological Museum: 1935, free. Open as Science Museum.
53 Victoria & Albert Museum: 1909. Collection started from items displayed at 1851 exhibition. Sculpture, furniture, silver, porcelain, costume, prints, drawings, ironwork and Constable paintings. Open Mon,Thu, Sat 1000-1750. Sun 1430-1750. Free.
54 Harrod's: 1895-1901, for fashionable shopping. Opened 1848 as small grocer's.
55 Lowndes Square: 1836-49. Doric and Tuscan porches.
56 Airways House: 1939. Passenger terminal of BOAC, now British Airways.
57 Eccleston Square: well laid out by T Cubitt 1835. No.25 is the Institution of Mechanical Engineers, founded 1873.
58 Victoria Station: built 1862 for the London, Chatham & Dover and London, Brighton & South Coast Railways. Tile map near ticket hall, Dover boat trains. Rebuilt 1909 and altered after 1923.
59 Westminster Roman Catholic Cathedral: 1903, Bentley. Early Byzantine style in redbrick and Portland stone. Holds 2,000. Lift to top of 273ft Edwards Tower.
60 Buckingham Palace: original 1703, remodelled by Nash 1813 and faced with Portland stone. Town residence of monarchs since Queen Victoria in 1837. Queen's Gallery open Tu - Sat 1100-1700, Sun from 1400. Free. Changing of the Guard ceremony most days at 1130.
61 Queen Victoria Memorial: figure 13ft high carved from one solid block of marble. 100ft radius semi-circular colonnaded screen.
62 St James's Palace: created by Henry VIII on site of 12thC. hospital. Only the gateway, Presence Chamber and 1532 Chapel Royal survived 1809 fire.
63 St James's Park: hunting park for Henry VIII. Landscaped with lake in 1829 by Nash. Surrounded by backs of Government offices: Admiralty, Paymaster General, Horse Guards, Treasury and Foreign Office.

64 No. 55 Broadway: London Trans-headquarters by Holden, 1929. Remarkable exterior sculptures by Epstein, Gill and Moore near top of west wing.

65 Central Hall: 1912. Headquarters of Methodist Church. 90ft diameter dome, seats 2,700. Here in 1946 was the first meeting of the UN General Assembly.

66 Dean's Yard: entrance has Gothic houses (1854), one with gatehouse enclosing Abbey gardens.

67 Westminster School: founded by Elizabeth I c.1560 as a successor to the monastic school.

68 Jewel Tower: 1365 and the only remaining part of the old Palace of Westminster. Once used to store the King's private fortune, now a museum. Open 1030-1600 daily.

69 Houses of Parliament: Royal Palace until 16thC. Westminster Hall 1097 at entrance with hammerbeam roof. Rest burned down and rebuilt in 1852 by Barry and Pigeon. Big Ben tower 320ft. Public galleries of Houses of Commons and Lords open during sittings. Free, but often long queues: try evenings.

70 Westminster Abbey originally built on island in river Tyburn with early Saxon church. Edward the Confessor founded the Abbey 1065. Mostly mediaeval. Twin west towers by Hawksmoor, 1740. Open 0800-1800, free.

71 Downing Street: official residences of the Prime Minister (No.10) and the Chancellor of the Exchequer (No.11). Built 1680, rebuilt 1964.

72 Horse Guard's Parade: colourful ceremonies including Changing of the Guard, most days at 1100. Inspection 1600.

73 Carlton Terrace: Nash, 1829. Links with his Regent's Park design via Regent Street. 1833 Duke of York's column.

74 Institute of Contemporary Arts: Nash house with exhibitions. Open Tu-Sat 1200-2000, Sun from 1400.

75 Admiralty House: 1786. 1760 screen by Robert Adam in front courtyard.

76 Trafalgar Square: by Barry 1829-41. 184ft Nelson's column 1843. Landseer bronze lions. Access difficult for inexperienced cyclists: walk round to see it all.

Adjacent: St Martin-in-the-Fields church, 1726 and Post Office open 0800-2000 daily.

77 National Gallery: founded 1824 with 38 paintings, now houses many famous works. Open 1000-1800. Sun from 1400. Free

78 National Portrait Gallery: founded 1856, Italianate building 1896. Royal portraits and others. Only one eighth of 5,000 collection on display. Open 1000-1700, Sun 1400-1800. Free.

79 Charing Cross Station: 1863, on site of Hungerford market. Hotel and Cross by Barry: an early use of artificial stone. Statue of Charles I on site of earlier cross erected by Edward I along the route of Queen Eleanor's funeral procession.

80 Southampton Street: laid out 1706 on site of Bedford House. YHA shop.

81 Covent Garden: by Inigo Jones, 1630, for Duke of Bedford. Market started 1670, halls built 1830-58. Fruit market moved to Nine Elms 1974, halls renovated 1980.

82 London Transport Museum: trams, buses and trains. Converted from flower market of 1889, and Jubilee Market 1904. Open 1000-1800 daily.

83 Royal Opera House: 1858, Barry. Frieze and statues saved from Smirke's 1809 building.

84 British Museum: 1823-47, Smirke. Archaeology and printing. Elgin marbles. Open 1000-1800. Sun from 1430. Free.

85 Montague Street: cast iron lamp bracket with ram's head motif, often used in Georgian design.

86 Church of St George: 1731, Hawksmoor. Splendid interior. On top of the steeple the lightning conductor is a figure of George I as St George.

87 Holborn Town Hall: 1906.

88 Lincoln's Inn Fields: laid out 1630-60. Nos. 59-60 on the west side date from 1640. Many of the other remaining mansions were built for the nobility in the 18thC Magnificent plane trees.

89 Sir John Soane's Museum: built by Soane 1812. Left with all its contents, including Hogarth paintings, on his death 1837. Open 1000-1700 Tu-Sat. Free.

90 Lincoln's Inn: one of three Inns of Court and the largest law library in London, founded 1474. Chapel 1623 with good stained-glass window and wood carvings. Old Hall 1506, gatehouse 1518. Open 1200-1400 Mon-Fri.

91 Star Yard: Victorian cast iron urinal.

92 Public Records Offices: contains the *Magna Carta*.

93 Dr Johnson's House: late 17thC, he lived here 1748-59. Compiled his Dictionary (published 1755) here. Open daily except Bank Holidays 1100-1700 (winter), 1100-1730 (summer).

94 St Bride's Church: 1670-84, Wren. On ancient site. Only steeple and font survived 1940 fire, but restored 1954. Museum in crypt, Roman altar.

95 Apothecaries Hall: 1684.

96 Youth Hostel: former St Paul's Choir School, 1875.

97 St Paul's Cathedral: rebuilt 1675-1710 by Wren. Dome, crowned with lantern and cross, rises to 365ft. Open daily 0800-1900, (summer) 0800-1700 (winter).

98 Guildhall: centre of City's government for over 1,000 years. Present building begun 1411. Gothic front built 1788-89. Roof and main hall rebuilt after war by Gilbert. Most extensive mediaeval crypt in London. Open Mon-Sat 1000-1700 Summer Suns 1400-1700

99 St Margaret: 1686-1700, Wren. Tower only remains.

100 Bank of England: founded 1694 to fund war against France. Present building 1937.

101 Royal Exchange: founded 1566, the present building was built in 1844 but is no longer used for Mercantile Exchange.

102 Mansion House: 1753-56, Dance.

The Lord Mayor of London's official residence.

103 Stock Exchange: founded 1773, rebuilt 1973, as 321ft tower block. Public gallery, open Mon-Fri 1000-1715.

104 Monument: to the Great Fire of London. Viewing platform open 0900-1740, Sun from 1400.

105 Customs House: rebuilt 1817 on 14thC site; Billingsgate Fish Market: 1873, cast iron. Market since 13thC.

106 Tower of London: includes 1078 White Tower. Open 0930-1700 (1600 winter) Mon-Sat. In summer Sun from 1400. Tower Bridge, 1894, now has electric bascules but is rarely raised.

107 Wakefield Gardens: remains of 10ft Roman City walls.

108 Trinity House: 1794, with Ionic columns. Rebuilt 1940 after bombing. Headquarters of lighthouses around Britain and Ireland.

109 St Olave: 1250, rare crypt *c*.1450. Pepys, who helped to save it from the 1666 Fire, is buried here. Restored after 1941 bombing.

110 No.42 Crutched Friars: elegant town house, 1725.

111 Fenchurch Street Station: 1854 facade. Electric trains to Tilbury and Southend upstairs.

112 Leadenhall Market: 1871. Retail market of 70 foodtrade shops in a complex of roofed footways beneath which lies the site of a Roman Basilica.

113 St Andrew Undershaft: 17thC windows show English monarchs and heraldry. Monument to J Stow with a quill pen in his hand which is renewed each year by the Lord Mayor.

114 St Helen's: mostly 13thC Sword rest 1665, belfry 17thC. Was attached to 13thC convent.

115 Cutler Street Warehouses: built 1769-1820 for the East India Company.

116 Petticoat Lane: interesting street markets, especially early Sunday mornings.

117 Artillery Lane: Georgian shop front.

118 Spitalfields Market: wholesale fruit and vegetables, founded 1682. Rebuilt 1928.

119 Christ Church: 1729, Hawksmoor. His biggest church in the centre of a conservation area and named after 1197 Priory of St Mary Spital. Money provided by 1711 Fifty New Churches Act intended to cater for growing congregations and combating non-conformist churches. Only eight churches were built under the Act. Being restored.

120 Finsbury Square: 1777-90. The first place to use gas for public lighting.

121 Whitbread's Brewery: 1774. Porter Tun room with spectacular timber roof. Tapestry of World War II on view. Open 1000-1700; Sun 1230-1800.

122 St Giles Church: reputed to have been founded 1090. Rebuilt c.1545, top of tower added 1883, burnt out during last war and rebuilt 1960. Surrounded by the Barbican development — named after the remains of a Roman watch tower — which is the City's main residential area.

123 Museum of London: Roman to 1930s, good displays. Open Tu-Sat 1000-1800, Sun from 1400.

124 St Bartholomew the Great: the oldest standing church in London, with a Norman Priory and Tudor gateway. Open daily 0900 to dusk.

125 Charterhouse: monastery 1371, school and home for old men 1611. School moved to Godalming, Surrey in 1872.

126 St Bartholomew's Hospital: founded with Priory 1123. Priory dissolved 1539. Henry VIII gave the hospital to the City and his statue (1702) is over the gateway.

127 Smithfield: world's largest meat market. Built 1868 on 'Smoothfield' site of St Bartholomew's. Fair and market since 12thC.

128 St John's Gate: built 1504, as entrance to Priory. The St Johns Order was suppressed in 1540 and most of the buildings destroyed. The Norman crypt and main gatehouse remain.

129 Clerkenwell Village Green: St James' Church 1788-92 by Carr, steeple 1849, renovated 1882.

130 Marx Memorial Library: built 1738 as a Welsh charity school.

131 Middlesex Session House: 1782, classical building but much altered.

132 Mount Pleasant Postal Sorting Office: built on rubbish tip of Great Fire debris, 1900-34. Private underground railway.

133 Field Lane Community Centre: built for 19thC slums by river Fleet. The river now flows in culverts from Hampstead to Blackfriars.

134 St Pancras Station: built 1868 with huge 243ft span train shed. The accompanying hotel, 1874, was almost too costly to build and is Gothic at its best. National monument, restored 1980. G Scott design.

135 Somers Town: former goods depot, being demolished for new National Library.

136 Woburn Walk: 1822, Cubitt. Early shop fronts.

137 St Pancras Church: 1822, the earliest of neo-Grecian designs.

138 Friend's House: 1927, Quaker headquarters.

139 Euston Station: 1968. Only the lodges on Euston Road remain of the 1836 station.

140 Tolmers Institute: built as a social centre for a poor area.

141 Regent's Park: a former Royal hunting park, laid out by Nash 1812-27 for a Royal Palace but opened to the public 1838. Regency terraces and four villas. Regent's Canal opened Paddington to Limehouse 1820, summer water bus to Little Venice. Roads opened to cyclists as a result of CTC action in 1885.

142 York Gate: Nash, 1811-27. Restored after bombing to offices.

143 Baker Street Station: important London Transport interchange, rebuilt 1928 and 1981.

144 Madame Tussaud's: waxworks exhibition. Begun in Paris with victims of French Revolution. Opened in Strand 1802, Baker Street 1835 and to present site 1884. Open daily except Christmas Day 1000-1700 or 1800. Combined ticket with adjacent London Planetarium, showing stars and planets.

145 Royal Academy of Music: founded 1822 and grants LRAM degrees.

146 St Marylebone Church: 1813-17, Hardwick. Large classical portico. The Brownings married here in 1846.

147 Wallace Collection: The Mansion, 1788. Works of art bequeathed to the nation on condition that the Government must provide buildings and upkeep. Exhibits to remain the same. Open 1000-1700, Sun from 1400. Free.

148 Welbeck Street: many fine 18thC houses.

149 St Peter's, Vere Street: 1721-24, Gibbs, to serve new estate around Cavendish Square.

150 St George's church: 1724; statues of hunting dogs on porch, probably from models by Landseer. Fashionable weddings.

151 Burlington Arcade: 1819, the first shopping arcade in England. Still retains regency atmosphere with Beadles on duty to enforce rules. 585ft long, 72 shops. No cycles.

152 Museum of Mankind: anthropological displays. Built 1860 as headquarters for London University. Open 1000 — 1700, Sun from 1430. Free.

153 Royal Academy of Arts, Burlington House: founded Pall Mall 1768, present site since 1869. Regular summer exhibitions 1000-1800, Sun from 1400. Also loan exhibitions January to March.

154 Saville Row: famous for fashionable tailors. Part of Burlington estate, developed from 1717.

155 Albany Flats: for batchelor gentlemen. Famous politicians have lived here.

156 St Anne's, Soho: 1803, Cockerell. Only tower remains after bombing. Dorothy L Sayers memorial.

157 Battersea church: 11thC, rebuilt 1775, gallery. Centre of a small village until the 1830s.

158 Albert Suspension Bridge: built 1878, incorporating new type of girder, patented 1858. Toll houses remain, but disused since 1879. One-way during rush hours, illuminated at night.

159 Cheyne Walk area: home of many artists, etc: Turner, Bellac, Brunel, Whistler, Adam. Mrs Gaskell was born here.

160 Carlyle's House: 1708. The historian lived here 1834-81, now a museum open 1100-1300, Sat 1400-1700 (Closed Tu). Cheyne Row is an elegant early Georgian terrace.

161 Carlyle Square: 1836-60, fine trees.

162 All Saints Chelsea Old Church: 13thC chancel, 16thC Thomas More Chapel. Rest bombed 1941. Open 0930-1300; 1400-1700 (not Tu mornings).

163 Christ Church: 1838. Pulpit 1786 from a City church.

164 The Royal Hospital: 1682, Wren. For veterans of the Civil War, its residents have long been known as the Chelsea Pensioners. Gibbons oak carving in chapel, 18thC Council Chamber by Adams. Chapel and Great Hall open 1000-1200 (not Sun) & 1400-1600.

165 Michelin House: 1910 art nouveau design with tile decorations.

166 St Augustine's: 1877, Butterfield. Angular design with coloured stone and marble.

167 Sloane Street: laid out 1780 by Henry Holland in honour of Sir H Sloane. Much rebuilt in 19thC.

168 Holy Trinity: 1890, Sedding-Burne-Jones window. Best examples of Arts and Crafts design in London.

169 Royal Court Theatre: rebuilt 1888, remodelled 1965. A bust of George Bernard Shaw is in the foyer at this theatre where his earlier plays were produced 1904-07.

170 St Barnabas Church: 1850, Cundy and Butterfield. Pioneer church in Anglo-Catholic movement. Bloomfield Terrace, Pimlico, early to mid 19thC.

171 Churchill Gardens: modern housing estate, 1946-62. Heated by hot water waste from Battersea Power Station. The first estate to be built with tall slabs mixed with tall terraces.

172 St James-the-Less: 1861, simple Gothic style. One of G E Street's most important churches. Fresco by Watts. Surrounded by 1971 housing.

173 Millbank Estate: 1902 for London County Council. First working class flats to be built as aesthetic and hygienic: art nouveau style doorway.

174 Tate Gallery: 1897. British

paintings from 16thC, modern foreign paintings, modern sculpture. Open 1000-1800, Sun from 1400. Free.

175 Smith Square: St John's, 1728, one of eight churches built under Fifty New Churches Act in 1728, restored after 1941 bombing. Baroque style. Transport House, Labour Party Headquarters to 1980, faces Conservative Central Office across square. Lord North Street has good Georgian terraced houses.

176 Department of the Environment: much criticised concrete and glass blocks: inappropriate but designed for Ministry of Housing in 1971.

177 Church House: 1940, Headquarters of General Synod of Church of England. Used as meeting place of Lords and Commons after 1941 bombing. UN Security Council HQ in 1945.

178 New Scotland Yard: 1967, Police headquarters.

179 Map Centre: Ordnance Survey agents.

180 Bluecoat School: 1709, brick building, founded 1688. Bought 1964 by National Trust and now used as office.

181 Royal Horticultural Association: founded 1804, the halls are often used for flower shows open to the public.

182 Lambeth Bridge: 1932, replaced the bridge of 1862 which was on the site of the Horse Ferry. Good view of Westminster.

183 Lambeth Palace: London home of the Archbishop of Canterbury since 1205, on the site of a Saxon manor house. 1495 gatehouse. Restored after 1941 bombing.

184 Albert Embankment: 1869, by the engineer Bazalagette. Good view of Houses of Parliament. St Thomas's Hospital, adjacent, moved here in 1868 when its original site was taken for London Bridge Station.

185 Westminster Bridge: 1862, replacing 1749 bridge. At the east end is a monumental lion of Coade stone, moved from the Lion Brewery when this was demolished. George VI joined in the appeal to save it.

186 County Hall: seat of the Greater London Council. Built 1912-33 in Portland stone on a granite and concrete base. Site of 1769 Coade stone factory: a hard wearing artificial stone used for many buildings until 1836 and made by firing china clay and glass.

187 Waterloo Station: The largest station in Britain, for Surrey and Hampshire. Also adjoining East station for Kent. Opened 1848, rebuilt 1922.

188 Railway Lift: for coaches of the Waterloo and City underground railway. No entry to station this way.

189 Shell Centre: 1962, a 351ft office block with public walkways at first floor.

190 Royal Festival Hall: one of the finest concert halls in the world. Opened 1951 for the Festival of Britain, seats 3,400.

191 Hayward Gallery: South Bank arts complex, 1968-76. Open 1000-1800 (Mon to Sat), 1200-1800 Sun. Cheaper on Mondays

192 Queen Elizabeth Hall and the National Film Theatre:

193 National Theatre: 1976. There are two main theatres, used for music, poetry, etc. Also exhibitions in the foyers.

194 Oxo Warehouse: 1932, with famous tower.

195 Kirkcaldy's Testing Works: 1873, could test-break iron bars of up to 20ft.

196 Horsetrough: one of many provided by the Association founded in 1859.

197 Cardinal's House and Provosts Lodging: 18thC View of St Paul's.

198 Bear Gardens Museum: 1000 to 1600 or 1700 Tu-Fri, 1300-1700 Sat & Sun.

199 Courage's Brewery: 1616, rebuilt 1962. 1852 fire plaque records links with Shakespeare's Globe Theatre and Dr Johnson's Anchor Inn.

200 Winchester House: the remains of a 1407 house owned by the Bishops of Winchester. Includes 1370 rose window. Amidst 19thC warehouses.

201 Southwark Cathedral: founded 1106 as priory church of St Mary Overe (over the water). 13thC design for present building, but much Victorian restoration.

202 George Inn: 1677. Part demolished in 1899 but theatre gallery remains. At the approach to London Bridge when that was the only bridge over the Thames. Coaching yards lined Watling Street nearby.

203 St Thomas's Hospital: now the Chapter House of Southwark Cathedral. Has the only semi-circular operating theatre in Britain, in use 1821-62. Open as museum 1230-1600 Mon, Wed, Fri.

204 London Bridge Station: terminus of London's first railway, to Greenwich, 1836. Recently rebuilt.

205 HMS Belfast: last of the battleships. Open 1100-1800, 1100-1630 winter. Expensive.

206 Hay's Wharf: An area reclaimed from the river for warehouses to serve ships in the Pool of London, the highest navigable point for large ships on the Thames. The shipping has now moved to Tilbury and there are controversial plans to build office blocks.

207 Courage's Brewery: founded 1789, rebuilt 1891 after fire. Shad Thames contains 19thC warehouses, mostly disused with rusting interconnecting bridges.

208 Connaught Chapel: 1810, Corinthian portico.

209 Macclesfield Bridge: where a gunpowder barge on the canal blew up in 1874. The split in the tree to the west can still be seen. The bridge was rebuilt with the columns reversed.

210 Central Mosque: 1978, golden minaret.

211 Primrose Hill: good views

212 London Zoo: founded 1826. Open 0900 (1000 in winter) to 1800 or dusk.

213 Open Air Theatre: summer performances since 1932.

214 Harley Street: leading physicians and surgeons practise here. The original buildings were plain Georgian, many remain c.1790.

215 London Telecom Tower: 580ft high, with restaurant (now closed), at top.

216 University College Hospital: founded 1833, rebuilt 1906.

217 University College: founded 1828 by J Bentham, free of church influence. Later incorporated into University of London.

218 Courtauld Institute: impressionist and post-impressionist. Open 1000-1700, Sun from 1400. Free.

219 Percival David Foundation of Chinese Art: ceramics collection. Open 1030-1700, not Sat pm, Sun or Mon am.

220 Coram Foundation: 1752. Open 1000-1600 Mon-Fri.

221 Her Majesty's Stationery Office: Government publications and guide books.

222 Old Curiosity Shop: 1567. Was probably a dairy when Charles II presented it to his Duchess of Portsmouth. Now an antiques shop. *NB:* Dickens' shop was another near Trafalgar Square.

223 Country Life Building: 1904. Lutyens 'Hampton Court' Renaissance.

224 Stanford's: British and foreign maps.

225 St Martin's Lane: mostly theatres and cinemas but also some 18thC houses.

226 Senate House: designed by Holden, with massive tower 210ft high. The administrative offices of the University of London and a library with a million volumes.

227 Bedford Square: 1776. The only 18thC London square surviving intact. Exteriors with stucco pilasters and pediments. Coade stone doorways.

228 Soho Square: 1681. No.1 Greek Street (House of St Barnabas) 1746 with finest interiors in Soho. Doric pilasters at No.50. No.48, 1742, first floor room with stucco ceiling.

229 Foyle's reputed to be the world's largest bookshop; one of the many in Charing Cross Road.

230 Lisle Street: 1791. Houses built in the gardens of Leicester House (1637-1790).

231 Leicester Square: laid out 1670. Centre of cinemas and theatres. Gardens purchased for the public 1874. Shakespeare statue of marble and around the garden are busts of Reynolds, Newton and Hogarth, who lived in or near the Square. Swiss Centre 1967.

232 Piccadilly Circus: Electric signs - best seen at night. Eros 1893 memorial to Lord Shaftesbury. Regent Street to north part of Nash's uncompleted link between Regent's Park and St James's Park. Mostly rebuilt in 1920s.

233 Our Lady of Assumption: chapel of the Portuguese embassy. Rebuilt with domestic front 1788, following the anti-Popery Gordon riots. Interior galleries.

234 Bourdon House: 1725, Tuscan pillaster panelling. A rare example of a still free-standing 18thC town house.

235 United States Embassy: originally laid out during George III's reign, but largely rebuilt over the last forty years.

236 St Mark's Church: rebuilt 1878, Blomfield. Victorian Renaissance style.

237 Grosvenor Chapel: 1730, part of the Grosvenor Square development.

238 Mount Street: 'A paradise of pink terracotta' says Persner. Largely rebuilt in the 1890s.

239 Hilton Hotel: 1963, a 300ft tower block for wealthy tourists.

240 Chesterfield Street: unusual in being entirely of Georgian terraces.

241 Berkeley Square: laid out 1675 as part of development of Hill Street and others to 1745. Some original houses remain, Nos. 1 and 44 being good examples. No nightingales now!

242 Royal Opera Arcade: 1818 by Nash and Repton. The only remains of the former Opera House, burnt down 1867. Bow-fronted shops.

243 Liberty's: 1924, timber-framed store. Mock Tudor, traditionally connected with advanced art and design.

244 All Souls' Church: 1822-4, Nash. Circular classical portico, thin spire. Bombed 1940, rebuilt 1951.

245 Broadcasting House: headquarters of the British Broadcasting Corporation and principal radio studios. Built 1931. Has the appearance of a ship.

246 St Mary's Bryanston Square: 1821-24, Smirke. 1875 alterations by Blomfield.

247 Marylebone Station: opened 1899 for the Great Central Railway, the last main line into London. Former Great Central Hotel now British Railways Board headquarters.

248 Park Village East: 1824, Nash. First 'model village' in a suburb. Canal arm behind used to serve hay market, partly filled with bomb rubble in 1945.

249 Former Carreras Factory: 1926. Still some traces of Egyptian Lotus style. Built on former Mornington Crescent Gardens, this building initiated the 1931 Act to stop building on London square gardens.

250 St Pancras Vestry House: administrative headquarters for the parish before the borough was formed.

251 Old St Pancras Church: Norman doorway, rest rebuilt 1848. Soane memorial, 1815, in eccentric style.

252 St Pancras Basin, Regent's Canal: formerly with coal shutes from railway. Area rebuilt 1868-70 for Midland and Great Northern Railways. Large King's Cross goods yard with tall granary, 1851. Much industrial archaeology.

253 Imperial Gas Works: Now much reduced in size but some gas holders remain: Rail workers' flats and Temperance Hall behind built 1870 for Great Northern Railway.

254 King's Cross Station: recently modernised but Cubitt's 1852 simple design still evident.

255 Lloyd Baker Estate: 1809-40, mostly heavy Grecian style.

256 Exmouth Market: a street market founded 1892, when Rosebery Avenue was opened as a bypass. Famous for jellied eels. Holy Redeemer church, 1888 Sedding Italian style.

257 Finsbury Town Hall: 1895, Flemish renaissance style.

258 Thames Water Authority: 1920, on site of New River head where London's first fresh water supply terminated in reservoirs at the end of a 38 mile canal, built 1613, from Hertfordshire.

259 Sadlers Wells: Founded 1683 with entertainment around the springs. 1765 music hall, rebuilt 1931.

260 Claremont Square: 1821, around 1709 reservoir, covered over 1856. Pentonville Road completed c.1770 as bypass for London together with Euston Road.

261 Chapel Market: 1790, street market since 1850s. White Conduit used to supply spring water to Charterhouse Monastery.

262 Cloudesley Square: 1825. Holy Trinity, 1829, Barry. Islington developed as a fashionable suburb but then declined until the 1960s. Now fashionable once more.

263 Thornhill Estate: 1829-52. Early shop front at corner of Barnsbury Road, sphinxes and obelisks on Richmond Avenue.

264 Agricultural Hall: 1862. Glass roof with 150ft span. Many controversial plans for demolition or reuse.

265 Camden Passage: late 18thC antique shops. Islington village grew around here from c.1735.

266 Duncan Terrace and Colebrooke Row: 1768, either side of the former New River. St John's 1843. Islington Regent's Canal tunnel 1816.

267 St Botolph: 18thC church by Dance.

268 National Postal Museum: includes 19thC Phillips collection of British stamps and registration sheets for almost every postage label since the Penny Black in 1840. Open 1000-1630 hrs Mon-Fri, 1000-1600 hrs Sat.

269 St Alphage House: a long section of City wall is preserved behind this building. Mediaeval and later work on a Roman base.

270 Liverpool Street Station: 1875, extended 1894. Built over a burial ground used as a plague pit in 1665. Hotel by Barry, tea shop on bridge linking platforms. Cathedral styling.

271 No.90 Curtain Road: a plaque commemorates the site of the first English theatre, opened in 1576 by James Burbage.

272 Spanish and Portuguese Synagogue: 1701, the oldest synagogue in England. Well preserved, 18thC fittings.

273 Toynbee Hall: founded 1884 by Oxford University social workers as a base for work to help the poor of the East End. War damaged.

274 Fashion Street: Moorish bazaar.

275 Truman Hanbury Brewery: 18thC and later.

276 Baroness Coutts Estate: c.1850, built as model dwellings. Also similar London County Council estate c.1890.

277 Shoreditch Church: 1740, Dance. Stocks adjacent.

278 Christ Church: 1838, Pennethorne Grecian style. Rossetti window, 1867. Galleried.

279 Poland Street Garage: supervised cycle parking.

4 SUBURBAN EXCURSIONS

Route 2
THE EAST END
20 miles (32 km) - round trip

OS: 1:50,000: 177 or London Street Atlas)

The east end of London is relatively seldom visited by tourists or people from other parts of the capital, yet it is an area of great interest and well worth exploring. There are, however, many busy roads and care is needed in selecting routes away from traffic. The routes shown do this as much as possible, as well as linking some of London's less well-known landmarks. The area is generally low lying.

a The towpath of the Regent's Canal from Stepney to Islington can be cycled by holders of BWB canal permits.

b Dismount to cross the railway by footbridge.

c Dismount to use pedestrian subway between Talwin Street and Three Mill Lane.

d The Northern Outfall Sewer is being developed as a cycle route to Beckton.

e Leave the Northern Outfall Sewer before the A11 bridge, cross that road by a subway and then follow the footpath to Pudding Mill Lane.

f There is a long flight of steps between the road and the Northern Outfall Sewer at this point.

g The route via Devons Road and Fairfield Road is very busy and the junctions with the A11 need particular care. The alternative route makes use of the Northern Outfall Sewer along which there is a rough path. This route does, however, require a certain amount of walking and the carrying of the cycle up or down a long flight of steps.

h Many of the roads in Victoria Park are closed to motors but all may be used by cyclists. Access to and from the park at some of the gates requires

dismounting. The park may be closed after dusk.

j Eastway is a busy road and the junctions near Molesworth gate complex.

k Dismount to use footpaths in this area.

l The perimeter path around Hackney Marshes is available as a cycle route, but during the summer the western path is also used by motor vehicles going to and from a camp site. Access to and from Millfields Lane is via a short private road belonging to the CEGB.

m Dismount to use short footpath next to church.

n Walk through doorway between Milner Square and Almeida Street.

A Spitalfields Market: wholesale fruit and vegetables. Founded 1682, rebuilt 1928.

B Christ Church: 1729, Hawksmoor. His biggest church in the centre of a conservation area and named after 1197 Priory of St Mary Spital. Money provided by 1711 Fifty New Churches Act, intended to cater for growing congregations and combating non-conformist churches. Being restored.

C Fashion Street: Moorish bazaar.

D Whitechapel Art Gallery: art nouveau entrance. Open Tu - Sun 1100 -1800 Free.

E Princess Alice PH: named after the pleasure steamer which sank off Beckton in the Thames after a collision which prompted the maritime rule of 'keep right' when passing other ships.

F Whitechapel Bell Foundry: founded 1570. Liberty Bell, Big Ben and the Kremlin bells were all cast here.

G London Hospital: founded 1740, the earliest surviving building dates from 1751.

H Trinity Almshouses: built 1695 for retired ships' masters. Restored after bombing.

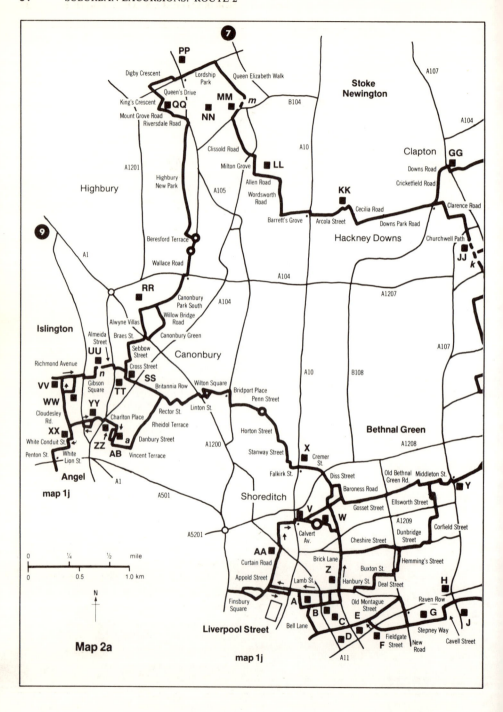

Map 2a

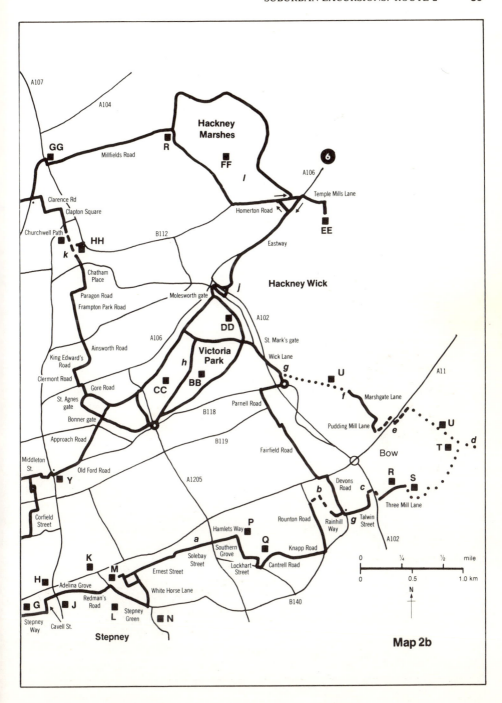

Map 2b

J Sidney Street: a famous name as the site of the 1911 seige when Churchill commanded the troops against armed gangsters.

K No. 81 Mile End Road: Spiegelhalters the jewellers shop remains surrounded by a department store.

L Stepney Green: some 18thC houses remain from the days when this was a select suburb.

M Maria Terrace: restored weavers' cottages. Note the large workroom windows upstairs.

N Stepney Parish Church: St Dunstan's, 15thC The east window shows 1940-45 bombing scenes.

P Hamlets Way: boundary markers between the Stepney and Poplar parishes remain on a wall.

Q Tower Hamlets Cemetery: opened 1841, but now largely overgrown.

R River Lea Navigation: an important water highway since Roman times, gradually enlarged for barges up to 87ft by 19ft. Still carries timber and metals, although some side channels are now abandoned.

S Three Mills: on the site of an ancient water mill. The present mills date from 1776 and 1817.

T Abbey Mills Sewage Pumping Station: part of Bazalgette's major sewage disposal scheme of 1868. The former steam pumps are now operated by electricity. Kremlin style in the east end. Visits can be arranged.

U Northern Outfall Sewer: a fully-enclosed sewer from Victoria Park to Beckton sewage works, with a path on top.

V Shoreditch Church: 1740, Dance. Stocks adjacent.

W Baroness Coutt's Estate: c.1850 model dwellings, adjacent to c.1890 London County Council estate.

X Geffrye Museum: situated in the heart of London's furniture trade, this museum of furniture is housed in the Ironmonger's Company's almshouses of 1713. Open Tu - Sat 1000-1700; Sun 1400-1700 Free.

Y Bethnal Green Museum: a branch of the Victoria & Albert with collections of toys, dolls, Spitalfields silks and sculpture. Open Mon - Thu & Sat 1000-1800; Sun 1430-1800.

Z Truman Hanbury Brewery: 18thC and later.

AA 90 Curtain Road: a plaque commemorates the site of the first English theatre, opened in 1576 by James Burbage.

BB Victoria Park: laid out by James Penethorne in 1842-45 on the site of Bonner Fields where Wesley preached. Land bought with the proceeds from the sale of York House (now Lancaster House) following a campaign to check the high death rate from disease in the East End due to the lack of open space.

CC Burdett Coutt's Fountain: a large monument to the woman who did much to help the poor of the East End.

DD Alcoves: 18thC, from the old London Bridge.

EE Eastway Cycle Track: venue for cycle racing.

FF Hackney Marshes: a large open space which is a footballer's delight: there are 110 pitches here.

GG Clapton Pond

HH Sutton House, Hackney: early 16thC house with panelling of various periods. NT.

JJ St John's Church: 1797, replacing an older church from which the tower remains to the SW. Greek style. Also stocks and whipping post from 1630.

KK St Barnabas: 1910 dark Byzantine block, hidden from street.

LL Cubitt Estate: 1830. Speculative housing by one of London's biggest 19thC developers.

MM Stoke Newington Churches: old mediaeval church replaced by 1853 Scott church on the opposite side of the road.

NN Clissold Park: the grounds of the 1820 Clissold House, now a public park with pets corner.

PP Green Lanes Pumping Station: 1856. Chimney disguised as a castle tower. Now at the end of the New River (see Route 7).

QQ Victorian Pillar Box

RR Canonbury Tower: Elizabethan country house built for a Lord Mayor of London. Only one wing remains and this is now used as a theatre. History on plaque at Nos. 1 - 7 Canonbury Place.

SS Little Angel Theatre

TT St Mary's Islington Parish Church: 1754, only the steeple survived bombing.

UU Milner Square: 1841. Peusner says 'disintegration of classical conventions'; Summeson 'an evil dream'.

VV Thornhill Estate: 1829-52. Early shop front at the corner of Barnsbury Road; sphinxes and obelisks on Richmond Avenue.

WW Cloudesley Square: 1825, Holy Trinity. 1829 Barry. Islington was developed as a fashionable suburb but declined until the 1960s. Now fashionable again.

XX Chapel Market: 1790. Street market since 1850s. White Conduit used to supply spring water to the Charterhouse Monastery.

YY Agricultural Hall: 1862, with a glass roof of 150ft span. Many controversial plans for re-use or demolition.

ZZ Camden Passage: late 18thC, with antique shops. Islington village grew from here from c.1735.

AB Duncan Terrace, Colebrooke Row: 1768, either side of the New River which is now culverted. St John's 1843, Regent's Canal tunnel beneath 1816.

Route 3
NORTHERN HEIGHTS
27 miles (43 km) - round trip

OS: 1:50,000: 176 or London Street Atlas
Bartholomew: *Everyone's London -* southern part only

This route is a guide to the north London 'villages' of Hampstead, Highgate, Hendon and Mill Hill. There are some steep hills on the various routes shown.

a Dismount to use footbridge over the Regent's Canal.

b Cycling is permitted on Hampstead Heath and Parliament Hill only on the paths shown. Give precedence to walkers.

c Cycling is only permitted on the path between Nassington Road and Highgate Road before 1000.

d Ashley Lane is a RUPP and therefore usable by cyclists. The surface is tarmacadamed throughout.

e It is necessary to dismount to cross the North Circular Road, which is very busy at this point. Take care.

A London Zoo: one of the largest and finest in the world.

B The Roundhouse: a former locomotive shed, built in the 1830s, now a theatre and arts workshop.

C Highgate Cemetery: contains the grave of Michael Faraday and the tomb of Karl Marx.

D Lauderdale House: 16thC Nell Gwynne was installed here by Charles II.

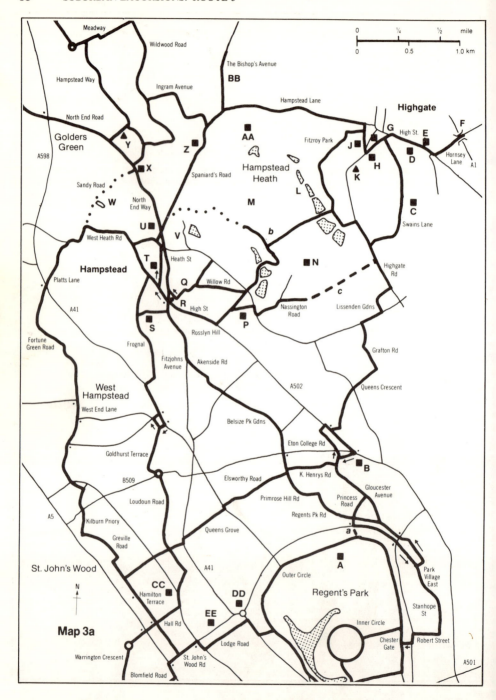

Map 3a

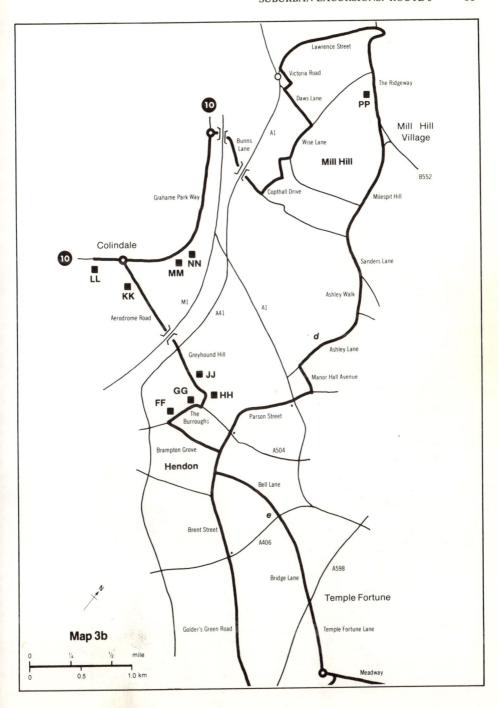

Map 3b

E Cromwell House: 1638. The connection with Cromwell is mythical, but there is a fine carved oak staircase and cupola.

F Archway: the road in the large cutting below was built in the 18thC to bypass Highgate Hill.

G Flask Inn: Famous public house, once patronized by William Hogarth.

H St Michael's Church: dominates the skyline for miles around. Coleridge is buried under the centre aisle and there is a modern east window of the Last Supper.

J The Grove: elegant 17thC and 18thC houses. No.3 was formerly the home of both Samuel Taylor Coleridge, poet and literary critic, and J B Priestley.

K Highgate Youth Hostel: the smallest of the London hostels.

L Highgate Ponds: constructed as reservoirs in Elizabethan times.

M Hampstead Heath: more than 800 acres and one of London's most effective 'lungs'. Famous fairs are held at bank holidays.

N Parliament Hill: a fine panorama over Central London can be seen from the top.

P Keats's House: preserved as a memorial to the poet. Open .

Q Flask Walk: Famous pubs lead to Well Walk where there is a drinking fountain over the spa spring.

R Hampstead Station: with platforms 192 feet below street level, it is the deepest on the Underground.

S St John's Church: the churchyard contains the graves of many famous people, including Hugh Gaitskell and Kay Kendall. Church Row is a tree-lined street with 18thC houses.

T Fenton House: 1693. Houses the Benton Fletcher collection of keyboard instruments and the Benning collection of porcelain and furniture. There is

also a delightful garden. NT, opening irregular.

U Jack Straw's Castle: an old public house, but extensively rebuilt after the last war.

V Vale of Health: a secluded hamlet within the Heath. Site of a small permanent fair.

W Leg of Mutton Pond: dug in the early 19thC by the unemployed poor of the parish.

X Bull and Bush: a popular public house, immortalized in song by Florrie Forde.

Y Hampstead Heath Youth Hostel: opened 1980.

Z Spaniard's Inn: an early 18thC inn with strong literary and historical connections. The highwayman Dick Turpin is reputed to have been a regular. Opposite is a preserved tollhouse at what was the entrance to the Bishop of London's park.

AA Kenwood House: built in 1616 by John Bill and remodelled as a 19thC gentleman's house by Robert Adam. One of the finest houses near London. Bequeathed by Lord Iveagh. Open.

BB Bishop's Avenue: a status symbol address. Some of the most expensive houses in London are here.

CC EMI Abbey Road Recording Studios: Origin of records by many popular singers and musicians, including The Beatles.

DD St John's Wood Chapel: 1813, Hardwick. Ionic portico, box pews.

EE Lord's Cricket Ground: headquarters of the Marylebone Cricket Club, the governing body for English cricket.

FF Barnet (Hendon) Town Hall: 1900

GG Middlesex Polytechnic in Hendon: 1937

HH Hendon Parish Church:
principally 13thC–15thC
with a fine carved Norman font and
13thC paintings.

JJ Church Farm House Museum:
17thC building. The ground floor is
arranged as it was in the 18thC and
there are changing exhibitions above.

KK Peel Centre: Metropolitan Police
training college, rebuilt during the
1970s.

**LL British Library Newspaper
Library:** an inexhaustible source of
reference material. Open upon
application.

MM Battle of Britain Museum:
opened in 1978, it includes a display of
the British and German planes involved
in the famous battle, with a number of
reconstructed scenes.

NN Royal Air Force Museum: this
museum traces the history of the RAF
and has a large collection of
representative aircraft. Opened in 1972.

The Battle of Britain and RAF
Museums, together with the housing
estate opposite, stand on the site of the
former Hendon Aerodrome. This was
opened in 1910 by Claude Grahame-
White as London Aerodrome and was
the venue for air displays until 1939.
The first United Kingdom air postal
service was inaugurated here in 1911.

PP Mill Hill School: founded in 1807
for boys of nonconformist families.
The large Gate of Honour is a war
memorial. There are fine views over
west London from further north along
The Ridgeway.

Route 4
HOUSES OF WEST LONDON
**25 miles (40 km) - round trip from
Putney**

05:1:50,000:176 or London Street Atlas

Here is a selection of routes linking the
historic houses and parks on both sides
of the Thames in west London. The

area is predominantly flat, but does
rise to 185ft (56m) on the west side of
Richmond Park.

*a Most of Lower Mall and Upper Mall
are footpaths and must be walked but
interesting old houses, pubs, etc. make
it worthwhile. A parallel cycle route is
under consideration and will be signed
if introduced.*

*b Because of the dangerous road
layout at the junction of Hogarth Lane
with Burlington Lane, it is recommended
that Hogarth House be left in the
direction of Park Road.*

*c The cycle path through Bishop's
Park closes after dark.*

*d A horse track and footpath subway
links the west side of Putney Hill with
the bridleway across Wimbledon
Common, enabling the A3 roundabout
to be avoided.*

*e The roads across the middle of
Richmond Park are closed to motor
vehicles but can be used by cycles.
Richmond Park closes at dusk.*

*f The road at Robin Hood Gate is one-
way into the park. To leave towards
the south, dismount and then walk to
Robin Hood Lane. This also avoids the
busy roundabout.*

*g Railhead Road leads to a short
riverside walk then to Ranelagh Drive,
Ducks Walk and Richmond Road.
Kilmorey Road and St Margaret's Drive
also lead to Ranelagh Drive.*

*h An occasional pedestrian ferry
service operates between Riverside and
Ham. There is also a footbridge to Eel
Pie Island.*

*j It is necessary to dismount and carry
cycles up to the footbridge across the
Thames at Teddington Lock.*

*k Cycling is permitted along the
Thames towpaths up-river from
Teddington Lock, except where notices
indicate otherwise.*

A Riverside Theatre: formerly
television studios, now a small theatre
offering plays, concerts, poetry, etc.

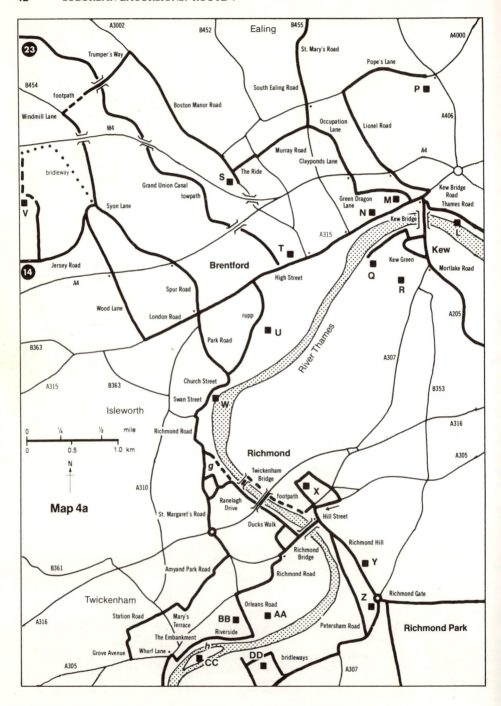

Map 4a

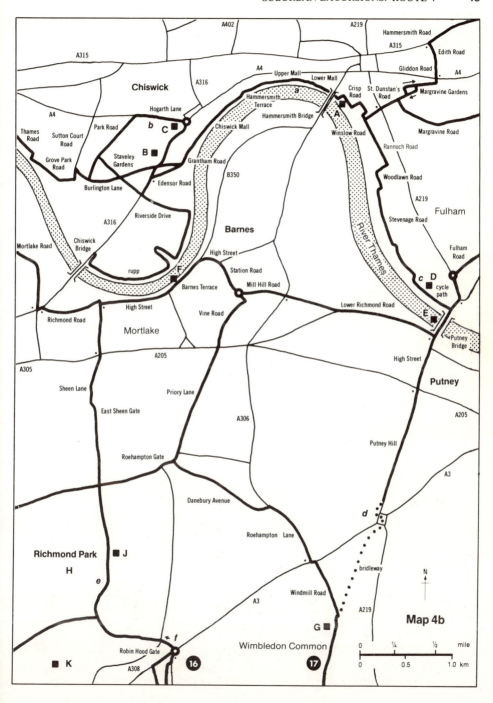

Map 4b

B Chiswick House: a Palladian villa built 1725-30 by the third Earl of Burlington a a meeting place for artists, writers and thinkers of the time. Open daily, except Mon & Tu October - March. DoE.

C Hogarth's House: a 17thC house, the home of Hogarth for 15 years and now a museum with paintings, drawings and other relics of the artist. Open daily except Tuesdays in winter.

D Fulham Palace: the former residence of the Bishops of London. The site of its former moat is now occupied by Bishop's Park.

E Putney Bridge: starting point of the annual Oxford and Cambridge boat race.

F Barnes: riverside terraces, a pond and a common.

G Wimbledon Common windmill: a smock and postmill, built in 1917 and restored in 1957.

H Richmond Park: this 2,500 acre Royal Park was once the hunting ground of Charles I and is now a natural open park with ponds and herds of wild deer.

J White Lodge: an 18thC Royal residence which is now a home for The Royal Ballet School.

K Isabella Plantation: a delightful woodland garden.

L Strand-on-the-Green: a waterside walkway lined with picturesque 18thC and 19thC dwellings. Well worth dismounting for.

M Kew Bridge Pumping Station: a steam museum with working engines and models together with an old workshop and forges. Open weekends.

N Musical Museum: a vast collection of instruments, musical boxes, gramophones, etc. Many are demonstrated during the one-hour long guided tour. Open weekend afternoons April to October.

P Gunnersbury Museum and Park: an early 19thC Rothschild mansion housing a local interest museum and Rothschild coaches. Open every afternoon.

Q Kew Palace: the former residence of George III. Open through Kew Gardens, but not of very special interest.

R Kew Gardens: these, the Royal Botanical Gardens, cover nearly 300 acres and are important as a centre for botanical research. The grounds contain an extensive collection of plants, trees, herbs, flowers, ferns, palms, etc. and there is also a tall Pagoda built in 1762 by Sir William Chambers. Open. (Cycles are not admitted but there are good railings at the north entrance).

S Boston Manor: an early 17thC house with fine plastered ceilings. Open Saturday afternoons, May to September.

T Brentford: the site of the first ford across the Thames that was always usable. The Butts is a charming tree-lined square with houses of different periods.

U Syon House and Park: an 18thC house - formerly Syon Abbey -with interior decoration by Robert Adam, fine furniture and portraits. Open Sunday to Thursday afternoons, June to September, and Sunday afternoons in Spring. Also extensive gardens, an aviary and an aquarium.

V Osterley House and Park: a 16thC Elizabethan house by Sir Thomas Gresham. Largely rebuilt in the 18thC, with some splendidly decorated rooms by Robert Adam. Open afternoons, except Mondays. NT.

W The London Apprentice: A 15thC Thames-side pub with Elizabethan and Georgian interiors. Contains prints of Hogarth's *Apprentices*.

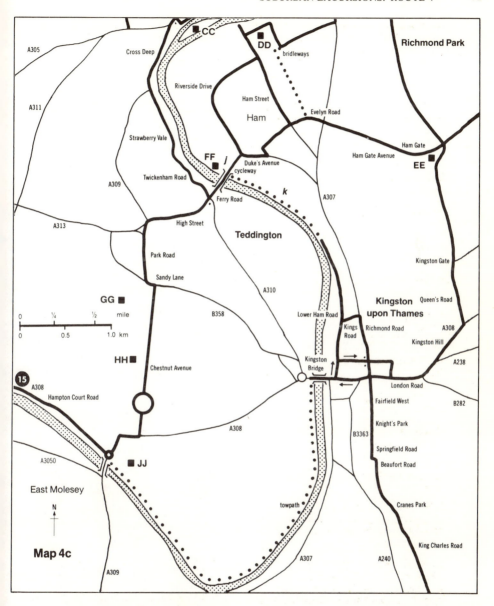

Map 4c

X Richmond Palace and Green: a little remains of the old palace built by Edward I and Henry VII. Many of the buildings around The Green - formerly the palace grounds - have regal connections.

Y The Terrace, Richmond Hill: a fine view over the Thames, as Turner painted it.

Z The Star and Garter Home: a home for disabled soldiers and sailors.

AA Marble Hill House: an 18thC. Palladian house built for the mistress of George II. It contains early Georgian paintings and furniture. Open daily all year.

BB Orleans House Gallery: most of the old house has been demolished but the 18thC. villa's fine Octagon Room, with elaborate stucco decoration, remains. The gallery also houses art collections and temporary exhibitions. Open afternoons, except Mondays, all year.

CC Eel Pie Island: once the site of a lavish hotel and nightclub, the island now contains luxury flats and houses. Accessible only by footbridge.

DD Ham House: a lavishly decorated 17thC. country house with collections of Stuart furniture. Open afternoons, except Mondays, from March to December. NT.

EE Ham Cross: an old CTC 'Caution: Cyclists take care' sign faces the cycles-only road to Spanker's Hill.

FF Teddington Lock and Weir: the end of the tidal section of the River Thames.

GG National Physical Laboratory: home of the UK time standard and an important centre for scientific research.

HH Bushy Park: Chestnut trees, deer and Diana's fountain lead to the Lion Gates of Hampton Court Palace.

JJ Hampton Court Palace: a great Tudor Palace built in the 16th century for Cardinal Wolsey and later given to Henry VIII. There are beautiful state rooms and paintings and vast gardens with the famous 'maze' and tennis court. Open daily.

**Route 5
SOUTH EAST LONDON
22 miles (35 km) - round trip**

OS: 1:50,000: 177 or London Street Atlas

This is a route which follows the little-frequented back streets by the Thames to Greenwich and then travels inland to the heights of Crystal Palace and the charming 'village' of Dulwich. The area is predominantly low lying except for some hills near Crystal Palace. The route maps also show the course of Route 20 through the suburbs and a useful bypass to the Elephant & Castle gyratory.

a Dismount to use footpath between Morgan's Lane and Shad Thames. Travelling west it will be necessary to walk along Tooley Street to avoid the circuitous one-way system.

b The area around Rotherhithe and the former Surrey Docks is being extensively redeveloped and changes may be made to roads, paths and sights.

c Dismount to use footpath over disused docks entrance.

d Service road behind shops avoids A200.

e Greenwich Park closes at dusk (1800 winter) when the alternative route via Maze Hill should be used.

f Many of the roads across Blackheath Common are closed at one end but these closures can be passed quite easily be cyclists. Take care crossing the A2 which is a very busy road.

g The route via Marsala Road is to be signed as a cycle route which will be much quieter than the A21.

h It is proposed to extend the Lewisham cycle route south to Catford and Beckenham Place Park.

j Dismount to use short, level footbridge over railway.

k Cyclists may use the direct road in Dulwich Park between College Road and Court Lane.

l The route shown is a signed cycle route to be introduced shortly.

m For cyclists, The Elephant & Castle gyratory is one of the most dangerous in London. Cyclists are advised to follow the bypass cycle route when this is available.

A HMS Belfast: the last of the heavy cruisers, now a floating museum. Open 1100-1750 (1630 winter), expensive.

B Hay's Wharf: an area reclaimed from the river to serve ships in the Pool of London. Nearby was the Pipe Borers' Wharf, where London's wooden water mains were bored between 1656 and the early 18thC.

C Potters Fields: cast iron bollards.

D Horsleydown Lane: bollards made from canon used in the Battle of Waterloo. The name is thought to be derived from Horse-le-down. The area was originally marsh but was drained by people of Belgic origin several hundred years ago to form pasture for cattle and horses. There are redevelopment plans for this area.

E Courage's Brewery: founded 1789 and rebuilt in 1891 after a fire. 19thC warehouses along Shad Thames are now mainly empty and connecting bridges rust.

F Maguire Street: 1905 London County Council pumping station.

G Fair Street: birthplace of Thomas Guy, founder of Guy's hospital and son of a lighterman and coal dealer. Livestock trading fairs were probably held here once. Nearby the western end of Druid Street was once Artillery Street, so named because it was built on a walled enclosure which has been used for the training of the 'trained bands' militia. The remains of St John's church, built 1737, are also near.

H Church of England Convent: a pleasing modern brick building.

J Jacob's Island: once a slum area, but now mostly demolished. The former Jacob's biscuit factory remains in Jacob Street, Vogans Mill at 17 Mill Street grinds soya, lentils, etc., and the former London Grist Mill is at 33 Bermondsey Wall West.

K St Mary Church: 1714, yellow brick with Corinthian columns.

L The Angel PH: *c.*1700. Ships waited here for space to enter the Pool of London and a village developed to serve their needs.

M Brunel's Engine House: used to pump water from the first Thames tunnel, started in 1825. Following flooding problems it opened in 1843 but the spiral approaches proposed for carts were never built. It was taken over by the East London Railway in 1865. The original steam pumps were replaced by electric in 1913. The engine house has been recently restored.

N Mayflower PH: said to have been the point of departure for America of the Pilgrim Fathers.

P Rotherhithe Tunnel: opened 1908. Steps lead down the ventilation shafts to the road tunnel below.

Q Surrey Commercial Docks: started 1809 and closed 1976. A principal cargo imported here was softwoods. The docks were also the starting point for the Surrey Canal. Begun in 1807 with visions of reaching Portsmouth, it never passed Peckham and has since been filled in.

R No. 265 Rotherhithe Street (Nelson's Wharf): an 18thC shipowner's mansion.

S Urban farm: with domesticated farm animals by old Docks entrance.

T Pepys Estate: a council housing development on the site of the Naval Victualling Yard founded by Henry VIII in 1513. Two buildings from 1780 have been converted into flats: 'The Colonnade', which were the old offices and 'Foreshore' which were once rum warehouses. Downstream was once the Deptford Dockyard, also established by Henry VIII, where Samuel Pepys was Clerk of Accounts 1658-73. The site was later occupied by the Foreign Cattle Market.

U Sayes Court: a manor given by William the Conqueror to Gilbert de Magnimot and now the name of a

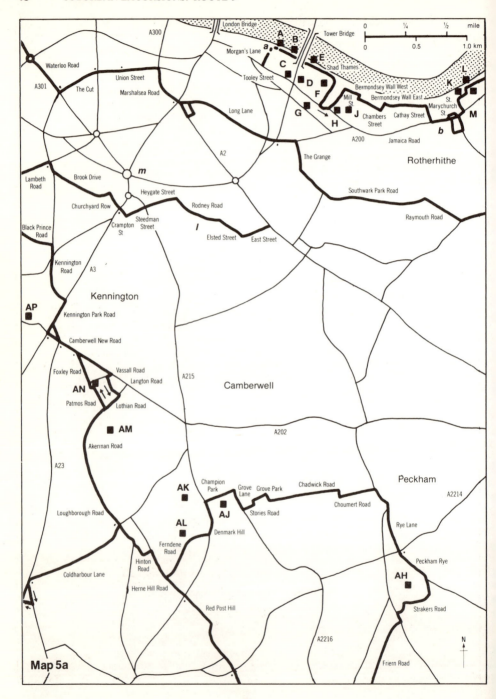

Map 5a

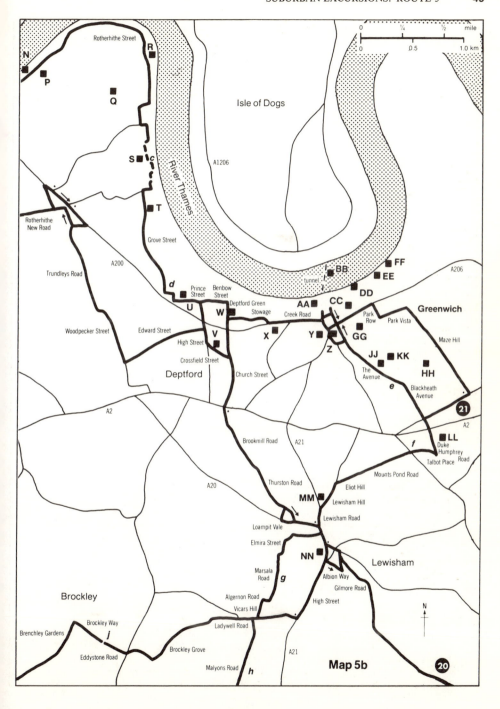

Map 5b

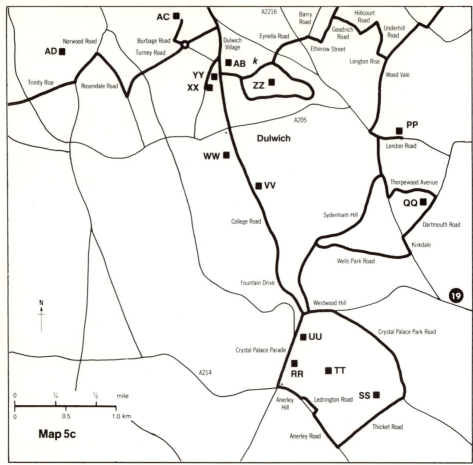

Map 5c

housing estate. John Evelyn the diarist also lived here. Nearby Czar Street is named after Peter the Great, Czar of Russia, who worked at Deptford Dockyard about 1698 as a carpenter.

V St Paul's Church: an imposing church built in 1730 by Thos Archer, a pupil of Wren. It has recently been restored.

W St Nicholas's Church: reputedly where Elizabeth I gave thanks for the defeat of the Spanish Armada. A brazier in the tower was once used for guiding shipping. The entrance portals of the churchyard carry a skull and

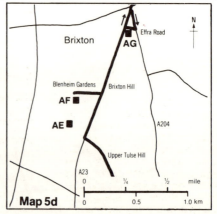

Map 5d

crossbones sculpture, an old time remembrance for the dead. This was later adopted as the sign of the many seamen who left here to take up piracy. There is a memorial to Peter Pett, inventor of the frigate, and others buried here include Christopher Marlowe, two sons of John Evelyn and Admiral Benbow. The pulpit is supported by a figurehead from the *Mayflower,* the mortuary is specially designed to prevent body snatching and there was once a plague pit too. This interesting church was rebuilt after damage in World War II.

X Deptford Creek: a lifting bridge allowed coal barges to reach the sewage pumping station, which pumps sewage into the Southern Outfall Sewer.

Y St Alphege Church: the traditional site of the martyrdom of the Archbishop of Canterbury in 1012. The present church was designed by Hawksmoor and contains the tombs of General Wolfe and Thomas Tallis.

Z The former Parthenon Theatre of Varieties is now a repertory theatre. There are some fine Georgian houses, including the Harbourmaster's House, and an enclosed vegetable market.

AA Cutty Sark: the last of the tea clippers, now in dry dock and open to visitors. Adjacent is the Gypsy Moth, the yacht in which Sir Francis Chichester circumnavigated the world single-handed.

BB Foot Tunnel to the Isle of Dogs: the constriction at the northern end was caused by a bomb during World War II. Cycles may be wheeled through.

CC Dreadnought Seaman's Hospital and Royal Naval College: built on the site of a royal palace in which several monarchs were born. The hospital closed in 1869 - by an Act of Parliament - and was then taken over as a naval college. Note the two large stone globes on the gateposts at the King William Walk entrance, which were adjusted to display the meridian,

latitude and longitude with great accuracy. The Painted Hall is worth visiting but is only open for two hours on Sunday afternoons. The name Dreadnought derived from a three-decker hospital ship moored off Greenwich.

DD Obelisk: commemorates Joseph Rene Bellot who perished in the search for Arctic explorer Sir John Franklin in 1853.

EE Trinity almshouses

FF Old houses and a riverside pub

GG National Maritime Museum: splendid collection of naval relics and models. The buildings include Queen's House, the oldest Italianate house in England, begun in 1617 by Inigo Jones for the Queen of James I.

HH Greenwich Park: a Royal park, first laid out by Charles II.

JJ Greenwich Observatory: established in 1765 but since transferred to Herstmonceux in Sussex. The buildings now house an astronomy and navigation museum. The meridian line and the imperial length standards are set into the wall and there is a time ball.

KK Bronze statue of General Wolfe: presented by the Canadian Government in 1930.

LL Blackheath Common: site of the gibbet on which malefactors were hung, gathering place for the rebels of Wat Tyler and where James I introduced the game of golf.

MM Obelisk: originally a drinking fountain, erected 1866.

NN Lewisham Clock Tower: built to mark Queen Victoria's diamond jubilee.

PP Horniman Museum: a fascinating museum of history and archaeology with special collection of carved furniture, armour and insects.

QQ Round Hill: the spire of Wren's City church of St Antholin Watling

Street. Once in the grounds of Round Hill House.

RR Crystal Palace: some remains can still be seen of the glass and iron palace built for the Great Exhibition of 1851 in Hyde Park and moved to Sydenham in 1854. The pleasure centre of south London, it was the most magnificent and costly building of its type ever built but was destroyed by fire in 1936.

SS Crystal Palace Park: once the grounds of the palace, it was restored as a public park in 1953 and includes life size models of prehistoric beasts as well as a small zoo and boating lake.

TT National Recreation Centre: a large sports centre for serious sportsmen. It is only open to members.

UU BBC Television Transmitter: the main transmitter for the London area since 1956. The mast was modelled on the Eiffel Tower.

VV Dulwich Toll Gate: a toll is still levied on motorists and drovers of sheep, cattle or ducks to help pay for the maintenance of this private road. Cyclists, however, go free.

WW Dulwich College, new buildings: 19thC but imitate 13thC Italian style in ornamentation. The school houses 700 boys.

XX Dulwich Art Gallery: open, with an interesting collection of paintings. The building also embodies a mausoleum containing the remains of the gallery's founders.

YY Dulwich College, original buildings: founded by Edward Alleyn in 1619 and designed by Inigo Jones. At one time the Master of the College had to have the surname Alleyn or Allen.

ZZ Dulwich Park: given to the public by the governors of Dulwich College in 1890. There is a lake, tennis courts, and open-air theatre.

AB Dulwich Village: still retains the character of a country hamlet.

AC Herne Hill Cycle Track: a venue for cycle racing.

AD Brockwell Park: the estate of Joshua Blackburn, bought for the public by a consortium of public bodies. The former mansions now serve as a refreshment house.

AE Brixton Prison: opened for women awaiting transportation, but now used only for men.

AF Brixton Windmill: built in 1816 and operated by wind power until 1862 and then by steam and gas. This tower mill was renovated by the London County Council in 1964, partly with machinery from a defunct mill at Burgh-le-Marsh in Lincolnshire. Open.

AG St Matthew Church: one of four churches in Lambeth built as a thanksgiving for the victory at Waterloo. The facade is adorned with large Doric pillars.

AH Peckham Rye Common: 'Rye' means common and this has been used for recreation since time immemorial.

AJ William Booth Memorial College: Salvation Army training college, opened in 1929.

AK King's College Hospital: founded at Clare Market in 1839 in connection with King's College and moved here in 1913.

AL Ruskin Park: a sundial marks the site of the house where Mendelssohn composed the popular Spring Song, originally known as Camberwell Green, in 1842.

AM Myatt's Fields: a public park on land formerly noted for its strawberries.

AN St John the Divine: a fine example of a Victorian church, built 1871-74 by Street and restored after war damage.

AP Oval Cricket Ground: home of the Surrey Cricket Club and shaped to match its name. The high walls make it difficult to see inside.

5. OUT-OF-LONDON ROUTES

Route 6
**LIVERPOOL STREET -
CHELMSFORD & COLCHESTER**
**31 miles (49 km) to Chelmsford or
63 miles (100km) to Colchester**

Bartholomew: 1:100,000: 15, 16
OS 1:50,000: 167, 168, 177

Liverpool Street - Hackney Wick:
for details of places of interest en route
see Route 2.

*a The route uses roads through
Victoria Park, most of which are
closed to motors but remain open for
cycles. Dismounting is necessary to
pass through Molesworth Gate, which
is adjacent to a busy junction. The
park may be closed after dusk.*

Leyton The church includes a bell cast
by Dawe about 1400.

Wanstead There is a 20ft marble
monument to Sir Josiah Child in St
Mary's church (1790).

Woodford Dr Barnado's home, near
the route, was established in the late
19thC to care for children from the
East End. At Woodford Green is a
statue to Sir Winston Churchill, local
MP from 1924 to 1964, and Hurst
House, an 18thC mansion with
Corinthian pilasters.

Chigwell The church contains a tablet
erected by London busmen to Britain's
first bus operator George Shillibeer.
William Penn was a pupil at the 16thC
grammar school.

Chigwell Row Hainault Forest, now a
GLC park, was once the hunting
ground of kings and abbots.

Navestock The church has beautiful
woodwork and a monument to James
Waldegrave, who was Prime Minister
for only five days in 1757.

Blackmore The church has a large
timber belfry rising in three stages and
capped with a shingled spire.

Writtle The birthplace of British
broadcasting as the site of Marconi's
first transmitter. There is a fine village

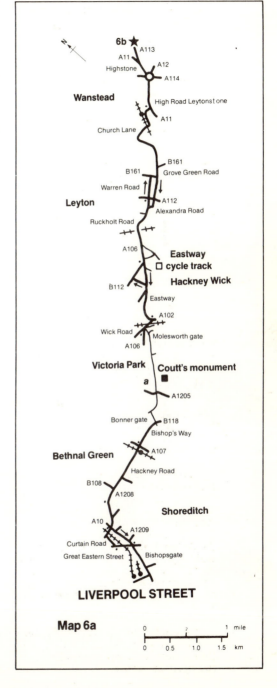

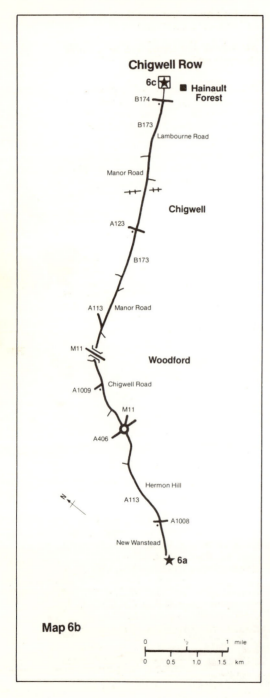

Map 6b

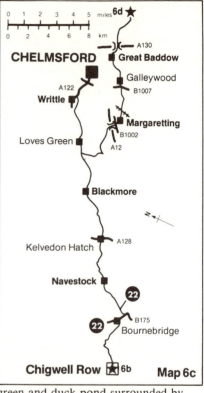

Map 6c

green and duck pond surrounded by Tudor and Georgian buildings. West of the village is 15thC Moor Hall, surrounded by a moat.

Chelmsford The church of St Mary has been a cathedral since only 1926 although the tower is 15thC. There is an interesting Chelmsford & Essex museum at Oaklands Park which includes items from a local Roman temple. The town had the distinction of being the first to light its streets with electricity.

Margaretting The beautiful church has a timber belfry and a rare Jesse window.

Great Baddow Old houses in winding streets; the church includes Roman tiles.

Danbury The highest hill in Essex, there are good views from the war

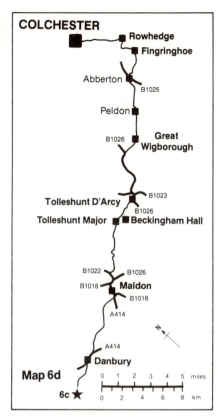

Map 6d

Beckingham Hall A 16thC hall with an interesting gatehouse.

Tolleshunt D'Arcy The 15thC church has battlements on the west tower and a good collection of brasses.

Great Wigborough In the tower hangs a piece of a girder of the Zeppelin which crashed here in 1916: the crew surrendered to the village constable.

Fingringhoe Thatched cottages and oak trees in a hollow by a pond. The church has mediaeval paintings.

Rowhedge Old fishing port.

Colchester The pre-Roman capital of SE England. The town has the most extensive Roman town wall remains in England and there are many buildings with Roman bricks. There is a museum to Roman Colchester in the castle keep, which is the largest Norman keep in Europe. There are also several other museums, including one of natural history in the former All Saints' church.

Route 7
ANGEL - EPPING FOREST
14 miles (22km)

Bartholomew: 1:100,000: 15
OS 1:50,000: 177

Angel, Islington see Route 2.

Stoke Newington Church Street is a mixture of dates and styles of buildings, one of the best of which is the pretty Sisters' Place, 1714. The west and east reservoirs, either side of Lordship Road, are now the end of Sir High Myddelton's New River, constructed in the early 17th century to carry water to London from the Amwell springs in Hertfordshire. Nearby in Seven Sisters Road, the public library contains the Chalmers Bequest of 18th century English paintings.

a Portland Avenue is closed at Clapton Common. Dismount to pass.

---

memorial. The Griffin Inn is a 16thC half-timbered building and there are beautiful 13thC oak effigies of the knights of St Clare in the church.

Maldon The old library at St Peter's church has a register recording the burial of George Washington's last English ancestor and also the christening of the captain of the Mayflower. All Saint's church has a window to Lawrence Washington, given by the town's American namesake. Interesting buildings include 13thC Beeleigh Abbey (open Wed afternoons) and the 15thC Moot Hall. Nearby is a sea-salt factory.

Tolleshunt Major Good views over the Blackwater estuary.

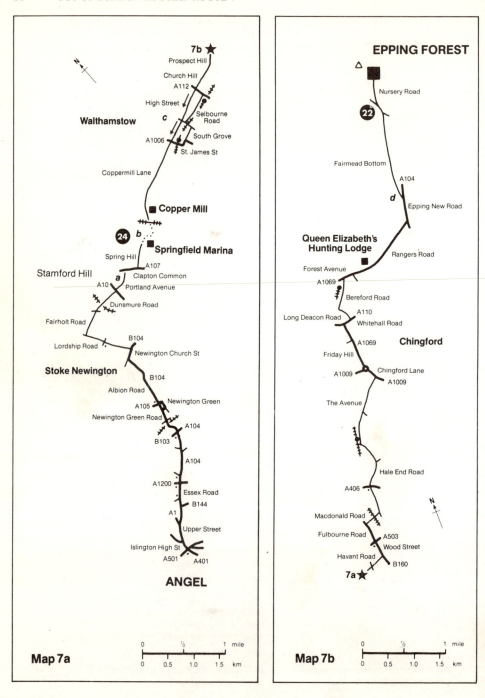

Map 7a

7b ★
Prospect Hill
Church Hill
A112
High Street
Walthamstow   *c*   Selbourne Road
A1006   South Grove
St. James St
Coppermill Lane

■ **Copper Mill**
24   *b*
■ **Springfield Marina**
Spring Hill
A107
Stamford Hill   *a*   Clapton Common
A10   Portland Avenue
Dunsmure Road
Fairholt Road
Lordship Road   B104
Newington Church St
Stoke Newington   B104
Albion Road
A105   Newington Green
Newington Green Road
A104
B103
A104
A1200   Essex Road
B144
A1   Upper Street
Islington High St
A501   A401
ANGEL

Map 7b

7b ★
EPPING FOREST
△ ■
Nursery Road
22
Fairmead Bottom
A104
d   Epping New Road
Queen Elizabeth's Hunting Lodge   Rangers Road
Forest Avenue
A1069
Bereford Road
A110
Long Deacon Road   Whitehall Road
A1069   **Chingford**
Friday Hill
A1009   Chingford Lane
A1009
The Avenue
Hale End Road
A406
Macdonald Road
Fulbourne Road   A503
Wood Street
Havant Road   B160
7a ★

0   ½   1 mile
0   0.5   1.0   1.5   km

0   ½   1 mile
0   0.5   1.0   1.5   km

b The Lea Navigation is crossed by a footbridge, following which there are two alternative bridges over the River Lea, one of which is sometimes barred. The track onwards is loose stone but easily rideable and is used by vehicles going to the nearby marina. The bridge under the railway line at the end of this track has very little headroom and dismounting is recommended.

Springfield Marina A popular centre for pleasure craft on the Lea Navigation.

Copper Mill Set up to strike copper coins during the Napoleonic wars, the building is now used as a water board storehouse.

Walthamstow The High Street is the venue for the largest open market near London. Around the church, off Church Hill, are several interesting buildings including The Ancient House. This 15th century timber framed building is now a shop. Vestry House museum nearby has excellent displays of local archaeology and history. Further north in Lloyd Park is a museum to the artist, poet, reformer and printer William Morris, who lived here as a child.

c On market days High Street is closed and the alternative route must be used in both directions.

Chingford The old church of All Saints, previously replaced by a new church on The Green and left to decay, was completely restored in 1928. It includes a 13th century arch and piers. On Pole Hill there is an obelisk, erected in 1824 as a north mark for Greenwich Observatory.

Queen Elizabeth's Hunting Lodge A timber framed three-storey early 16th century hunting lodge, now a museum of Epping Forest's history. Open most afternoons.

d Fairmead Bottom is closed at the A104 and the last few yards of the old road have been obliterated save for a footpath which is easy to miss.

Epping Forest The remains of a great forest which once covered much of eastern England. The present forest was preserved for the use of the public by an Act of Parliament in 1871. It is administered by the Corporation of London and is the largest open space under the guardianship of a public body in England. At Ambersbury Banks there are the remains of an Iron Age fort covering 12 acres.

Route 8
ST PANCRAS - HARLOW
28 miles (45km)

Bartholomew: 1:100,000: 15
OS 1:50,000: 166, 167, 176

Highgate, Archway see Route 3

a The main route follows the old racecourse road which is now available as a cycleway. The surface is stony but firm. The old road starts to the right of the main vehicle entrance at Hornsey Gate end and on the left inside Wood Green gate. The alternative route follows the main park road, climbing to Alexandra Palace from where there are extensive views.

Alexandra Palace The first palace was built in 1873 as a rival to Crystal Palace in south London but was burnt down only a month after opening. The replacement building, opened in 1875, was much less lavish but served as a major entertainments and exhibition centre for a further century. The great hall contained a huge organ by Willis. Alas, fire struck again in 1980 completely destroying the Great Hall and other buildings. In 1936 the BBC inaugurated the world's first high definition public television service from the NE wing of the Palace and this continued to be a television centre, latterly for Open University programmes, until 1981. In Alexandra Park the remains of former terraces and a racecourse can be seen.

b Use the subway to cross Sterling Way, A406.

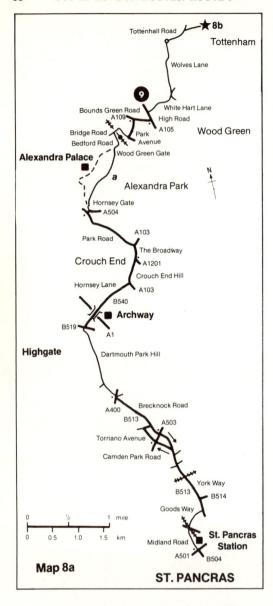

Map 8a

ST. PANCRAS

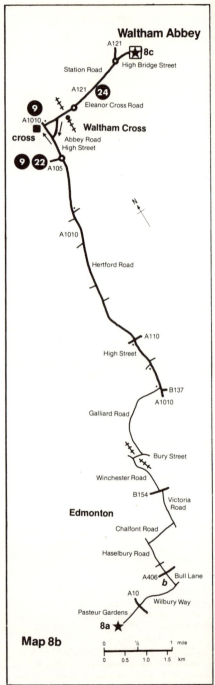

Edmonton Now mainly a residential area to the west with industry along the Lea valley, the town grew up along the old Hertford Road, A1010, where some old buildings still survive. Salisbury House in Bury Street, was once a manor house, built around

Map 8b

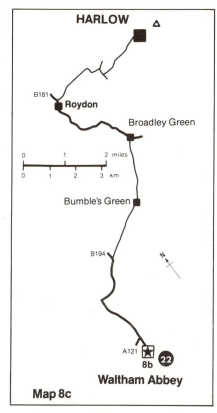

Map 8c

HARLOW

B181

Roydon

Broadley Green

Bumble's Green

B194

A121
8b 22

Waltham Abbey

1600, but is now used as an arts centre. The overhanging building has a timbered front and plastered sides. Pymmes Park was once the site of a house belonging to Lord Burghley. The park includes an attractive walled rose garden.

Waltham Cross The cross is one of only three survivors of 12 set up by Edward I to mark the resting places of his dead queen Eleanor when she travelled from Harby to Westminster Abbey in 1290.

Waltham Abbey The church is one of the finest examples of Norman architecture in the country, founded in 1030 although the present remains date largely from the 12th century. King Harold, who had consecrated the church, was buried here after the Battle of Hastings. The abbey, from which the town takes its name, was

built by Henry II, but only the present church survives. Sir Edward Poynter painted the brilliant nave ceiling and Thomas Tallis was organist here during the 16th century. Waltham Abbey is the centre of a large market gardening area.

Roydon Stocks and an old lock up on the green.

Harlow The new town, established in 1947, is one of the most successful of those built to relieve London after the war. Encompassing four former villages, the chief planner was Sir Frederick Gibberd. The town possessed the first pedestrian precinct in the country and also has a cycle path network. The old town to the north was the site of a Romano-Celtic temple and theatre. The interesting buildings which survive include The Gables and The Chantry, 16thC, some 17thC almshouses and fine 18thC houses around Mulberry Green.

Route 9
ANGEL - SAFFRON WALDEN & CAMBRIDGE
50 miles (81km) to Saffron Walden, 68 miles (108km) to Cambridge

---

Bartholomew: 1:100,000: 15, 20
OS 1:50,000: 154, 166, 167, 176

Angel, Islington see Route 2

a The route uses carriageways in Finsbury Park, which are open to cyclists in their entirety. Dismounting is necessary at Seven Sisters Road in order to pass through the Park gates.

Finsbury Park Opened in 1869, this is an occasional venue for cycle racing events.

Enfield A town with many fine old houses, expecially in Gentleman's Row. Charles Lamb lived for a time at No. 17. The church of St Andrew in the market place is interesting, with a 13thC chancel window.

b Forty Hill is closed at its southern end and dismounting is necessary.

Forty Hall Built in 1632 for Sir Nicholas Raynton, then Lord Mayor of London, this is a charming house surrounded by beautiful gardens,

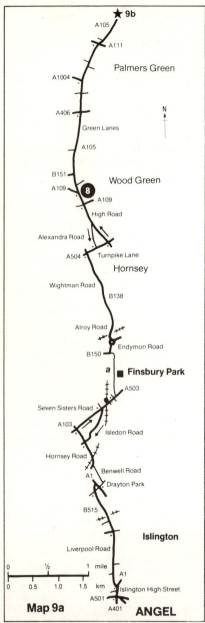

Map 9a   ANGEL

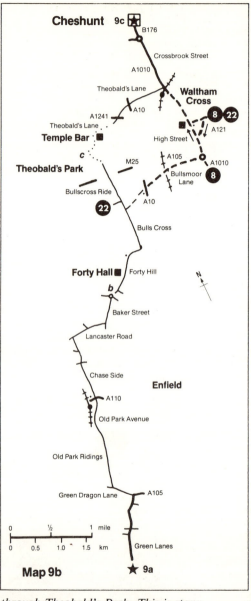

Map 9b

which include tall cedars and a lake. The hall is now a cultural centre and museum (open).

c The main route follows a bridleway *through Theobald's Park. This is stony but generally rideable and the few muddy stretches after wet weather can usually be passed without difficulty. The alternative route follows busy roads, but avoids the A10.*

Theobald's Park Little remains of the old palace of Theobalds built for Lord Burghley but exchanged with James I for Hatfield House. East of the road is Theobald's Park College, now a school.

Temple Bar Erected as one of the main gates into the City of London in 1672, it was moved to its present site in Theobald's Park in 1887. The Bar is now surrounded by a high fence and heavy foliage to curtail vandalism, but there are plans for its return to the City of London once more.

Waltham Cross see Route 8.

Cheshunt Lying in the Lea Valley, nearby there are 1,000 acres of glasshouses in which are produced a quarter of Britain's salad crops. The area is also popular for angling and boating on the river and in the many disused gravel pits.

Hertford The county town, is comparatively unspoilt by new roads. The town centre has a Victorian Corn Exchange, a handsome building with decorated plaster work, and the Shires Hall, built in 1769, was designed by Robert Adam.

Standon St Mary's church, 13thC, has a large west porch and a detached tower unique in Hertfordshiree. It is built into the hillside and has three levels. Two miles north-east at Standon Green End, a stone commemorates the landing of Vincenza Lunardi by balloon in 1784. He was the first traveller in England to arrive from the skies. Upp Hall nearby has a spectacular barn with original 17thC pointed arched openings.

Braughing An important village since Roman times, when it was at the hub of seven roman roads, including Ermine Street and Stane Street. There is an interesting 15thC church and half-timbered house with 16thC moulded plasterwork.

Furneux Pelham The 13thC church has windows by Morris and Burne-Jones and an inscription painted around the clock on the tower: 'Time Flies - Mind Your Business'.

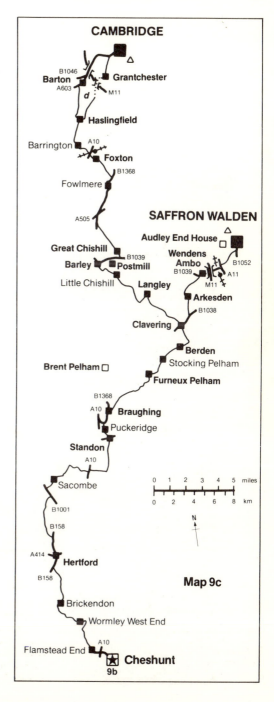

Brent Pelham Mediaeval stocks and a whipping post.

Berden Interesting buildings include Berden Hall, 16thC, with a wide handsome staircase, and Berden Priory, also 16thC which uses two ancient coffin lids for doorsteps and has a treadmill. The village church, part 13thC, has a beautiful pulpit and a luxurious chancel.

Clavering A scattered village, the lane leading to the church is particularly picturesque. Nearby are the earthwork remains of a Norman castle and some lovely old cottages. The church itself includes fine 15thC glass. NW of the village are two old windmills.

Arkesden A very pretty village with a stream running alongside the road. The church is rich in ancient monuments.

Wendens Ambo The name means 'both Wendens', from the joining together of two former villages in the 17thC The church includes medieval paintings on the theme of the life of St Margaret. Adjacent is Wenden Hall, an attractive farm.

Audley End House (DoE, open) The present building is the remains of a Jacobean palace, once so vast that it was never completely furnished nor fully occupied. The great hall includes a magnificent oak screen. Audley Park, laid out by 'Capability' Brown in 1736, includes other fine classical buildings and there is a round temple on Ring Hill and a stately Adam bridge over the river Cam.

Saffron Walden A town of great beauty, it is dominated by its church, the largest in Essex: 184ft long, 80ft wide with a spire 193ft high. There are many fine timbered houses in the town, including the youth hostel (owned by the NT). The Sun Inn (also NT), a many-gabled building, is now an antique shop, but was the headquarters of Cromwell and Fairfax in 1647. There are also attractive almshouses from the 14th and 15thC. The interesting local museum, near the castle, includes a collection of humming birds. On the common at the east of the town is one of the few surviving town mazes in the country and is at least 300 years old.

Langley Thatched and timbered cottages and a 17thC hall, now used as a farm.

Barley A village with pretty overhanging cottages. The 'Fox and Hounds' is 300 years old and the 'Big House' at Shaftenhoe End is of interesting appearance.

Great Chishill The post mill beside the road from Barley was built in 1819 and is well worth a visit. The key can be obtained from a nearby cottage.

Foxton Many thatched cottages and a 13thC flint church.

Haslingfield Chapel Hill is only 215ft high but gives a superb panorama of the Cam valley and much of Cambridgeshire as far as Ely Cathedral. Some 80 village churches can be seen on a clear day. Haslingfield church has a fine 15thC tower.

d The route via Grantchester avoids main roads but includes the use of a bridleway, which can be muddy after wet weather.

Barton On the Roman Akeman Street, the church has a Norman piscina and font, framed with a beautiful tower arch. There is also an interesting collection of wall paintings.

Grantchester A serene village of thatch, timber and plaster, once the home of the poet Rupert Brooke. Two miles SW are the eight giant dishes of the world's largest telescope.

Cambridge Established as a Roman town by AD70, Cambridge is now a busy commercial centre and one of the world's foremost seats of learning. Many of the colleges can be visited, as can King's College Chapel, world famous for its music and containing Ruben's painting *The Adoration of the Magi*. The city is rich in museums and has a splendid botanical gardens. Industries include radio and electronics and the manufacture of scientific instruments.

Route 10:
MARBLE ARCH - ST ALBANS
26 miles (42 km)

Bartholomew: 1 : 100,000: 15
OS 1 : 50,000: 166, 176

*a Marble Arch gyratory is hazardous
for cyclists. For avoiding routes
connecting with this route, see the
Central London maps (Route 1).*

*b The alternative route along the A5 is
more direct and easier to follow, but is
usually very congested. If using this
route, avoid the hazardous roundabout
at Staples Corner (A406 junction) by
using the lower flyover, signed A5.*

*c The route between Templehof
Avenue and Layfield Road is via the
shopping centre access road and the
emergency exit from the first car park
on the left going north. Riding south,
turn right leaving the car park.*

*d The alternative route is more direct
and preferable if it is not intended to
visit the aircraft museums.*

**Newspaper Library, Peel Centre,
Battle of Britain Museum, RAF
Museum:**see Route 3.

Edgware A modern suburb based on
an old stage-coach halt. The
picturesque old forge, now a gift shop,
in High Street is reputed to have been
the inspiration for Handel's *The
Harmonious Blacksmith.* Handel
composed many of his famous works
at St Lawrence Church in nearby
Stanmore.
*e The northern part of Edgwarebury
Lane is an RUPP. It has an uneven
surface, but is generally easy to ride.*

Elstree World renowned as the home
of British films, the studios are in fact
a mile away in Borehamwood.

Aldenham Country Park Based on
Aldenham reservoir which was built to
feed the Grand Junction (now Union)
Canal. Sailing, nature trails, etc.

Elstree Aerodrome Popular with
amateur pilots: busy at weekends.

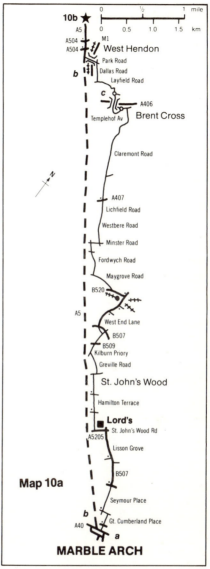

Letchmore Heath An attractive
compact village.

Aldenham Beautiful Norman Church
with fine oak screen. Aldenham House
is famous for its gardens.

Radlett The modern church includes
fine carvings of past monarchs,
preserved from its predecessor.

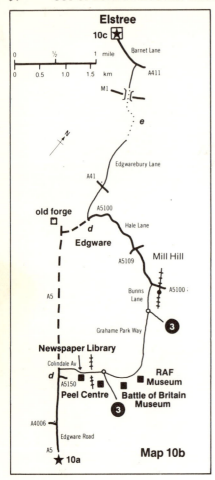

Map 10b

g The narrow bridleway along the south side of the River Colne is generally easy to ride and provides an attractive alternative route.

St Albans 16thC Abbey with the highest Norman tower in England; only Roman municipality *(Verulamium)* and most extensive remains in Britain; old houses; mediaeval belfry in High Street. Town now famous for printing. Guidebook essential.

Environs: Gorhambury, one mile west: remains of home of Francis Bacon (buried at St Michael's church) next to 18thC home of Lord Verulam, complete with ten Corinthian columns. Childwick Green, two miles north: attractive secluded village. Rideable bridleway from A5 roundabout.

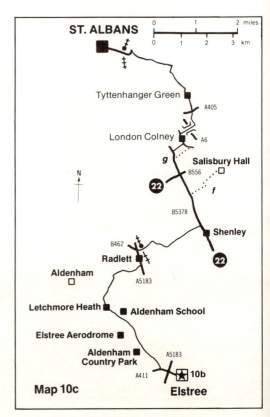

Map 10c

Shenley Grave of Nicholas Hawksmoor, an architect who worked on St Paul's Cathedral, Blenheim and many other famous buildings, in the churchyard.

Salisbury Hall 16thC country house with moat by Sir John Cuttes. Open Thursday and Sunday afternoons in summer. Also Mosquito Aircraft Museum.

f The bridleway from Shenleybury to Salisbury Hall is easy to follow, but is well used by horses and can be muddy after wet weather.

Route 11
NOTTING HILL - LEE GATE & IVINGHOE
36 miles (57 km) to Lee Gate,
43 miles (69 km) to Ivinghoe

Bartholomew: 1:100,000: 15
OS 1:50,000: 165, 166, 176,

a A signed cycle route is proposed between Neasden and Draycott Avenue which will include a bypass to the Neasden underpass. Signs will indicate when this route is available.

Wembley Complex The Empire Stadium, built for the 1924-5 British Empire Exhibition, is famous as the venue for English football Cup Finals. Also part of the Wembley Complex are the Empire Pool, used for ice skating, horse shows and other sporting events, and the new Exhibition and Conference Centre.

Harrow On Harrow Hill are 18thC houses, the parish church, whose 13thC spire is visible over a large area, and Harrow School. The school, founded in 1572 but with buildings from many periods, is one of the most prestigious schools for boys and past pupils have included Sir Winston Churchill, Lord Byron and Sir Robert Peel.

Ruislip St Martin's Church (High Street), part 13thC, contains mediaeval wall paintings and a bread cupboard for the poor dating from 1697.

Harefield Picturesque 17thC almshouses. The church of St Mary the Virgin has an impressive interior with many monuments, brasses and coats of arms. The burial ground also has much of interest. Although in Greater London, this area is still primarily agricultural.

b Long Lane has been cut in two by the M25, but there is a through bridleway link with a stony surface suitable for cycling.

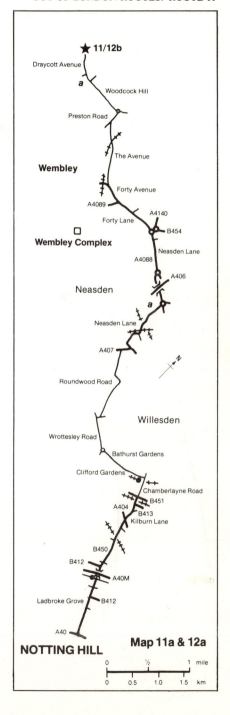

Map 11a & 12a

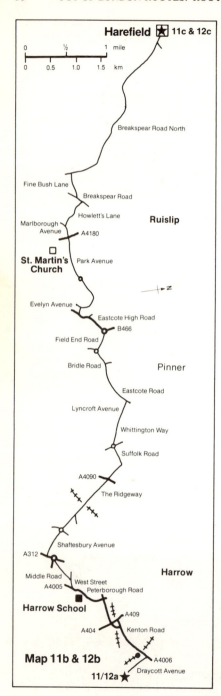

Map 11b & 12b

Chenies A neat village with a manor house, the former home of the Dukes of Bedford (open). The 15thC church contains interesting brasses and the attached Bedford Chapel has memorials to the Dukes' families.

Chesham Church Street (B485) has many buildings of architectural interest, including The Bury: a fine 18thC red brick mansion.

The Lee South of the village at a bend in the road is an old ship's figurehead of Earl Howe. At Lee Gate there is an old church with a William Cromwell window.

Latimer Small fairy-tale village green with a horse's grave near the war memorial.

Flaunden A Victorian church, originally designed by Sir George Gilbert Scott.

Berkhamsted Ancient castle ruins (DoE, open) The Grand Union Canal passes through the town.

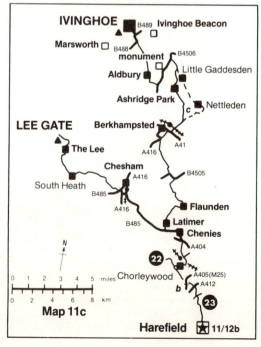

Map 11c

c The alternative route, through pleasant villages, can be used if the road through Ashridge Park is closed.

Ashridge Park The 16thC manor house is now a training college and has fine gardens (NT). The surrounding Berkhamsted Common (NT) has many acres of fine woodland and there is a tall monument (open) to the third Duke of Bridgewater who was a pioneer of English canals. There are good views from the the top.

Aldbury A pretty village, complete with duck pond, stocks and a whipping post. There is a timbered manor house and a church containing monuments, brasses and a mediaeval stone screen.

Marsworth: The Grand Union Canal has a series of locks here and to the south lie two reservoirs which are also nature reserves. Much canal machinery was once made at Bulbourne, nearby.

Ivinghoe The church has a fine roof, carved mediaeval pews and an iron firehook attached to the wall. The youth hostel was formerly a brew house. Nearby are Pitstone post mill (1627) - the oldest dated windmill in England - and Ivinghoe Beacon, a hill commanding fine views.

Route 12
NOTTING HILL - JORDANS & OXFORD
27 miles (43 km) to Jordans, 71 miles (113 km) to Oxford

Bartholomew: 1:100,000: 14, 15
OS 1:50,000; 164, 165, 175, 176

Notting Hill - Harefield: for details of places of interest en route, see Route 11.

a A signed cycle route is proposed between Neasden and Draycott Avenue which will include a bypass to the Neasden underpass. Signs will indicate when this route is available.

Chalfont St Giles Cottage Museum to the poet John Milton.

Jordans Famous Quaker meeting house with the grave of William Penn. Nearby is the Mayflower Barn, constructed of timber from the famous ship.

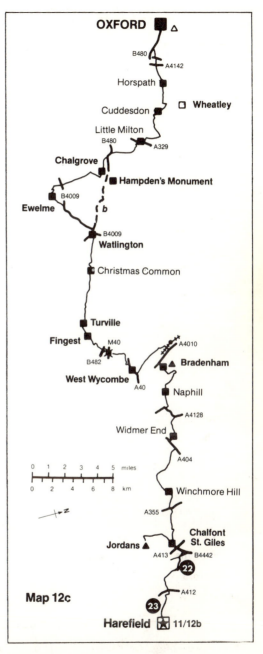

Bradenham The manor house was the boyhood home of Benjamin Disraeli.

West Wycombe Old village (NT). The hilltop church has a huge gilded ball on its tower which, with the caves below (open), was once used as a meeting place for the Hell Fire Club. The Palladian manor house is set in ornamental gardens (NT, open June to August).

Fingest Fine church with a twinned tower.

Turville A tiny village green flanked by a small Norman church and flint-faced cottages. There are also some picturesque half-timbered and thatched buildings and, on the hilltop, a restored windmill.

Watlington 17thC market hall.

b The alternative route, along the B480, can be used as a short-cut if time is pressing.

Ewelme The fine 15thC church contains much of interest including the perfectly preserved tomb of Alice, Duchess of Suffolk. Jerome K Jerome, author of *Three Men in a Boat,* is buried in the churchyard. With the old almshouses and village school, the church makes a delightful group. The village is also the centre of a thriving watercress industry.

Chalgrove A pretty village with thatched buildings and two roadside streams. The 12thC church has some 14thC wall paintings. Nearby at Chalgrove Field, the site of a Civil War battle, is a monument to John Hampden, whose refusal to pay Charles I's ship tax precipitated the war.

Wheatley Parish pit and lock-up.

Oxford The University, founded 1214, has many colleges and some are open to the public. There are also many other fine buildings including libraries, museums and theatres. Christ Church Cathedral dates in part from the 8thC, but is mainly 12th - 14thC. Oxford is the home of Britain's oldest botanical gardens, founded in 1621.

Route 13
NOTTING HILL - HENLEY
40 miles (64km)

Bartholomew: 1:100,000: 15 or 9
OS 1:50,000: 175, 176

a The alternative route avoids the M41 roundabout when riding west, and is signed for cyclists. It is not, however, practical to avoid the roundabout riding east and extra care should be taken.

Acton Once 'the farm by the oak trees', this suburb is now dominated by industry.

Ealing The 'Queen of the Suburbs'. Interesting buildings nearby include the Town Hall (Uxbridge Road), Pitshanger House, now the central library backing Walpole Park and Ealing Studios. The latter were once the home of British comedy films, but are now used for television.

Yeading A modern residential suburb. St Edmund's church in Yeading Lane (off route) has fine furnishings.

Cowley Peachey The 12thC church was the smallest in the former county of Middlesex. The bellcote, added in 1780, is of timber with a leaded spire.

b The River Colne is crossed by a short footbridge.

Iver An interesting church, the Saxon nave of which includes Roman bricks. Nearby are some delightful old houses.

Pinewood Film Studios Opened in 1936 by J Arthur Rank, the studios have more recently been famous for the James Bond extravaganzas.

Stoke Poges The village in which Thomas Gray composed his immortal *Elegy.* His writing room at Stoke Court (formerly West End Cottage) has been preserved and there is a large monument (NT) to him $\frac{1}{2}$ mile (1km) south of the village. The graveyard, where Gray is buried, is one of the most visited in Britain, as is the village church which is entered by a fine

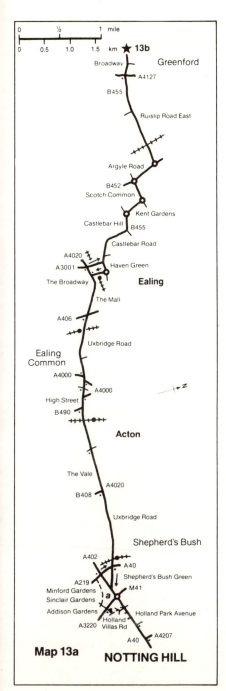

Map 13a

0   ½   1 mile
0   0.5   1.0   1.5   km   ★ **13b**

Broadway
A4127

B455

Ruislip Road East

Argyle Road

B452
Scotch Common

Kent Gardens
Castlebar Hill
B455
Castlebar Road

A4020
A3001   Haven Green
The Broadway   **Ealing**
The Mall

A406

Uxbridge Road

Ealing Common

A4000
A4000
High Street
B490

Acton

The Vale
A4020
B408

Uxbridge Road

Shepherd's Bush

A402
A40
Shepherd's Bush Green
A219   M41
Minford Gardens
Sinclair Gardens   *a*
Addison Gardens
Holland Park Avenue
A3220   Holland Villas Rd
A40   A4207

NOTTING HILL

Greenford

Map 13a

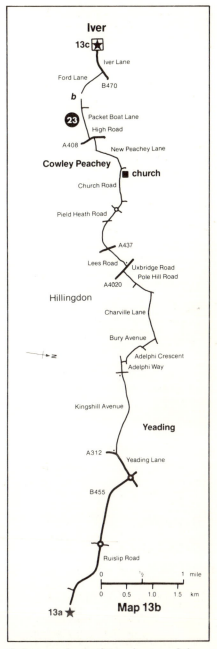

Iver
13c ✪

Iver Lane
Ford Lane
B470
b

23   Packet Boat Lane
High Road
A408   New Peachey Lane
Cowley Peachey   ■ **church**
Church Road

Pield Heath Road

A437

Lees Road
Uxbridge Road
Pole Hill Road
A4020

Hillingdon

Charville Lane

Bury Avenue

Adelphi Crescent
Adelphi Way

Kingshill Avenue

Yeading

A312   Yeading Lane

B455

Ruislip Road

0   ½   1 mile
0   0.5   1.0   1.5   km

13a ★   **Map 13b**

timber porch. A picture in one of the
13thC stained-glass windows of a

velocipede is one of the earliest portrayals of a bicycle yet found. The manor house in Stoke Park has royal connections and there is a tall monument in the grounds to a former occupant, Sir Edward Cole.

Burnham Beeches This area of natural woodland, now largely owned by the Corporation of London, is unique for the antiquity of its trees. Some beeches are nearly 1,000 years old.

Bourne End Fine sailing reach.

Cookham An attractive village around a green. The church contains *The Last Supper* by Stanley Spencer, who lived locally. Around Cookham is one of the finest lengths of the Thames. Nearby is Cliveden House (NT, open weekend afternoons in summer; gardens daily), once a meeting place of the famous.

Marlow Once the home of the Shelleys and Izaak Walton; also there is a fine

19thC suspension bridge over the Thames and a whipping post, stocks and an old prison door on the green.

Medmenham The church has an interesting timber chancel. There are charming cottages, an inn and a manor house and the remains of St Mary's Abbey.

Henley-on-Thames Venue of the famous Royal Regatta every July, this is a pleasant town with an attractive 18thC five-arched bridge and timbered houses, including 14thC Chantry House. The main street is Georgian and the town has many old inns and an active independent brewery.

Route 14
WEST BROMPTON - HEATHROW AIRPORT & WINDSOR
15 miles (24km) to Heathrow Airport
23 miles (36km) to Windsor

Bartholomew: 1:100,000:9
OS 1:50,000: 176

West Brompton - Osterley House: for details of places of interest en-route, see Route 4.

a The main route uses minor roads and is more interesting but includes a section to be walked. The alternative route uses busier roads and is longer in distance, but would probably be quicker.

b The section from Crisp Road to Upper Mall is a footpath and must be walked. A parallel cycle route is under consideration and may be introduced subsequently.

Heston The site of an early airfield; the area is now mainly residential.

Cranford The small Round House in the High Street was used to imprison thieves.

Harlington The church, $\frac{1}{4}$ mile ($\frac{1}{2}$km) north of the route, has a superb Norman doorway and the only Easter sepulchre in Middlesex. The stump of a

Map 14a

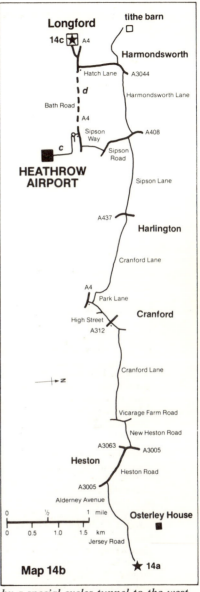

Map 14b

1,000 year old yew tree is in the churchyard. Much of this area is still devoted to market gardening.

c Cyclists must enter Heathrow Airport by a special cycles tunnel to the west of the main vehicle tunnels. Approach is via a cycle track which starts at a roundabout off the A4 200yds (200m) west of Sipson Way. Leaving the airport, signs direct cyclists to the start of the cycle track.

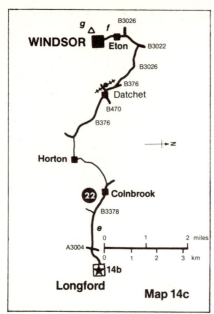

Map 14c

Heathrow Airport The site of an airfield since 1929, the present civil airport was opened in 1946. There are four terminals and five runways. A roof garden on the Queen's Building is open to the public and gives good views over the operating areas.

d The alternative route via Bath road is very busy. Extra care is also necessary where the main route crosses this road, especially when riding east.

Harmondsworth Large 500 year old tithe barn, still used for storing grain.

e There are general traffic restrictions along the B3378 at the approach to Longford and through Colnbrook village. These do not apply to cycles and any misleading signs should be ignored.

Colnbrook Formerly an important staging post on the old Bath Road. Several old inns. Cox's Orange Pippin apples first grown (1845) on Bath Road on Stanwell side of Colnbrook.

Horton Early home of John Milton. The church has a magnificent Norman doorway.

Eton Famous public school founded by Henry VI in 1440. Former pupils have included 19 British prime ministers. The library includes many literary treasures such as the 15thC Mazarin Bible and St Mary's Chapel contains rare wall paintings dating from 1479. There are guided tours in summer. Eton High Street contains many craft and antique shops, some of great age. A 15thC cockpit survives near old stocks and a Victorian postbox.

f The bridge linking Eton with Windsor is closed to motors but can still be used by cyclists. Ignore all traffic signs to Windsor as these lead via a much longer and very busy route.

Windsor The castle, founded by William the Conqueror in 1070 and open to the public, is the largest inhabited castle in the world and the present Queen's favourite residence. There is much of interest including the state apartments, Queen Mary's Dolls' House and St George's Chapel. The Changing of the Castle Guard takes place at 1025 daily. In the town the Guildhall, by Sir Christopher Wren, dates from 1689 and Church Street contains many 17thC and 18thC buildings, including Nell Gwynne's House and the Old King's Head. The Household Cavalry Museum is open daily and nearby is Windsor Great Park where cyclists may use many roads closed to other traffic.

g Windsor Youth Hostel can be reached by following the Thames via Barry Avenue and Stovell Road. Cycleways link sections closed to motors. This route avoids busy roundabouts.

**Route 15
PUTNEY BRIDGE - ENGLEFIELD GREEN
24 miles (38km)**

Bartholomew: 1:100,000: 9
OS 1:50,000: 176

Putney Bridge - Hampton Court: for details of places of interest en route, see Route 4.

a The route uses roads through Richmond Park which are closed to motor vehicles. Richmond Park closes at dusk, after which time the alternative route should be followed. This is, however, via very busy roads.

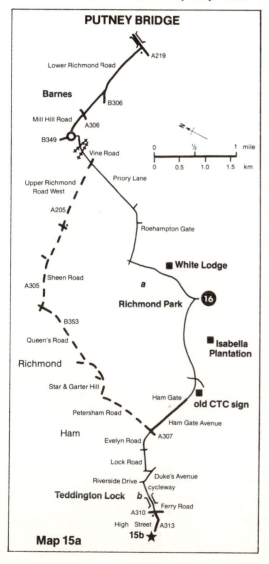

PUTNEY BRIDGE

A219
Lower Richmond Road
Barnes
B306
Mill Hill Road
A306
B349
Vine Road
Upper Richmond Road West
A205
Priory Lane
Roehampton Gate
■ **White Lodge**
a
Sheen Road
A305
Richmond Park
16
B353
Queen's Road
■ **Isabella Plantation**
Richmond
Star & Garter Hill
Ham Gate
■ **old CTC sign**
Petersham Road
Ham Gate Avenue
Ham
Evelyn Road
A307
Lock Road
Riverside Drive
Duke's Avenue cycleway
Teddington Lock   *b*
Ferry Road
A310
High Street
A313
15b ★

0   ½   1 mile
0   0.5   1.0   1.5   km

Map 15a

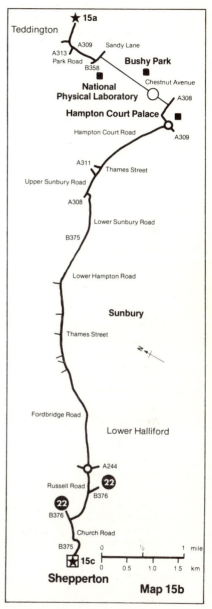

★ **15a**
Teddington
A309   Sandy Lane
A313
Park Road   **Bushy Park**
B358
Chestnut Avenue
National Physical Laboratory
A308
Hampton Court Palace ■
A309
Hampton Court Road
A311   Thames Street
Upper Sunbury Road
A308
Lower Sunbury Road
B375
Lower Hampton Road
Sunbury
Thames Street
Fordbridge Road
Lower Halliford
A244
Russell Road   **22**
22   B376
B376
Church Road
B375
★ **15c**
Shepperton

0   ½   1 mile
0   0.5   1.0   1.5   km

Map 15b

b Dismount to use footbridge over the Thames at Teddington Lock.

Sunbury Thameside views and a weir.

Shepperton Pleasing 17th-18thC

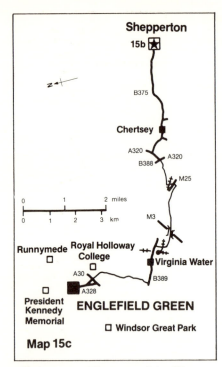

Shepperton

15b ⊠

B375

Chertsey ■

A320

A320

B388

M25

0   1   2 miles

0   1   2   3   km

M3

Runnymede □   Royal Holloway College □

⚡ Virginia Water

A30

B389

□   A328

President Kennedy Memorial   **ENGLEFIELD GREEN**

□ Windsor Great Park

Map 15c

village centre. The start of the Wey Navigation is nearby (NT).

Chertsey 7-arched 18thC bridge over the river. There is a museum, a few remains of a Benedictine Abbey and a Curfew Bell in the church, weighing more than 1 ton.

Virginia Water An affluent residential district. The long lake of the same name is 1½ miles (2km) west and was created in the 18thC by the Sandby brothers.

Royal Holloway College A huge 'chateau', modelled on Chambord for local pill millionaire Thomas Holloway in the late 19thC. Richly decorated.

Windsor Great Park Includes the Savill Garden, with plants of botanical and horticultural interest, and the Valley Gardens. Cyclists may use all roads in the Park.

Runnymede Site of King John's sealing the draft of the *Magna Carta*

in 1215. There is a memorial on Cooper's Hill. NT.

President John F Kennedy Memorial Dedicated to United States Air Force men killed in the Second World War. Nearby is a cenotaph to Commonwealth airmen and this has a viewing tower.

Englefield Green A modern hamlet around a green on the edge of Windsor Great Park. There are many places of interest nearby.

Route 16
PUTNEY BRIDGE — HOLMBURY ST MARY & GODALMING
33 miles (53 km) to Holmbury St Mary, 39 miles (63 km) to Godalming

---

Bartholomew: 1:100,000: 9
OS 1:50,000: 176, 186, 187

Putney Bridge - Richmond Park for details of places of interest en route, see Route 4.

a The route uses roads through Richmond Park which are closed to motor vehicles. Richmond Park is closed at dusk, after which time the alternative route should be followed. This route is, however, via very busy roads.

b The road at Robin Hood Gate is one-way into the park. To leave, dismount and then walk to Robin Hood Lane in order to avoid the busy roundabout.

c Use the service road adjacent to the A3. Approach from the north via Robin Hood Lane, leave to north onto A3 just before roundabout.

d Dismount to use short footpath.

Chessington Large open-air zoo.

e The alternative route is via a bridleway through the wood, which is rideable at all seasons.

Cobham Mill by River Mole, Cedar House (NT: open only on prior application), Yew Cottage gardens. The timbered 15thC Church Stile House has a rare double overhang.

Telegraph Hill Ruins of signal post which, with 12 others, was used to send semaphore signals to the Fleet at Portsmouth in the 19thC.

Ockham The Hautboy Hotel was where Lady Harberton, a cyclist, was refused service in 1898 because she wore 'rational dress'. The subsequent court case, when Lady Harberton was given legal backing by the CTC, was

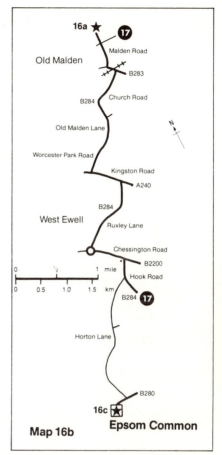

Map 16b

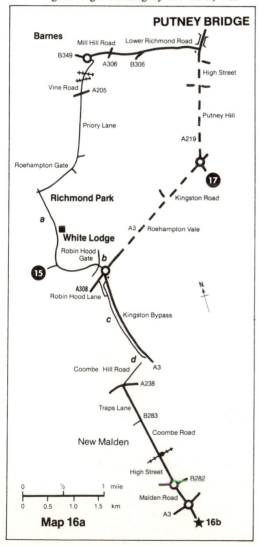

Map 16a

an important landmark in women's struggle for equal rights.

East Clandon Timbered cottages, old barns, church with shingled spire. Hatchlands Georgian house (NT, restricted opening).

Shere Attractive village with 12thC church. The 'Silent Pool' is one mile west on the A25.

Abinger Hammer Village clock with a smith striking a bell; working smithy.

Abinger Stocks, whipping post and old houses.

Friday Street Beautiful hamlet with a lake, amongst wooded hills and approached by narrow lanes.

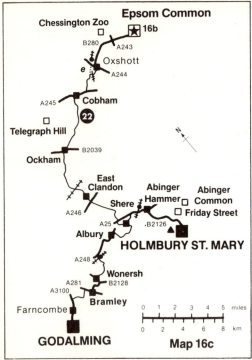

Map 16c showing route through Chessington Zoo, Epsom Common, 16b, B280, A243, Oxshott, A244, A245, Cobham, 22, Telegraph Hill, B2039, Ockham, East Clandon, Shere, A246, A25, Abinger Hammer, Abinger Common, Friday Street, B2126, HOLMBURY ST. MARY, Albury, A248, Wonersh, B2128, A281, A3100, Bramley, Farncombe, GODALMING

Holmbury St Mary Leith Hill, at 965 feet the highest point in south-east England, is nearby.

Albury Albury Park (open) has gardens laid out by John Evelyn, the diarist.

Wonersh Once the centre of Surrey's cloth industry. Many old houses and a lovely church.

Bramley Delightful Unstead Bridge nearby.

Godalming Old wool town and half-way stop on the old London to Portsmouth coach route. Narrow streets and half-timbered houses. The 'Pepperpot', former town hall, is now a local history museum. Charterhouse School, with mock Gothic buildings, lies above the town. Winkworth Arboretum (NT: open all year), with rare trees and shrubs, is three miles south-east. Since 1966 the Headquarters of the Cyclists' Touring Club has been in the Godalming suburb of Farncombe, in Meadrow.

Route 17
PUTNEY BRIDGE - GATWICK AIRPORT
28 miles (45 km)

Bartholomew: 1:100,000: 9
OS 1:50,000: 176, 187

a The route via Wimbledon Common is largely traffic-free and more pleasant but uses loose stone tracks. A horse track and footpath underpass avoids

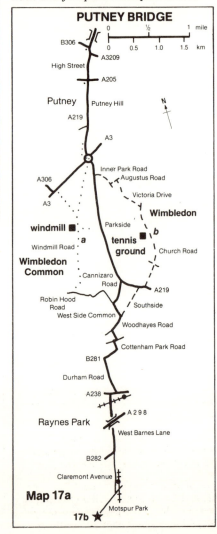

Map 17a showing PUTNEY BRIDGE, B306, High Street, A3209, A205, Putney, Putney Hill, A219, A3, Inner Park Road, Augustus Road, A306, Victoria Drive, A3, Wimbledon, windmill, Windmill Road, Parkside, tennis ground, Church Road, Wimbledon Common, Cannizaro Road, A219, Robin Hood Road, Southside, West Side Common, Woodhayes Road, Cottenham Park Road, B281, Durham Road, A238, A298, Raynes Park, West Barnes Lane, B282, Claremont Avenue, Motspur Park, 17b

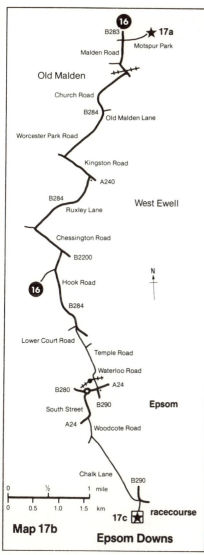

Map 17b

Epsom Downs

Wimbledon Common Smock and post windmill, built in 1817 and restored in 1957. Iron age fortifications at Caesar's Camp.

Epsom A former spa, now famous for its racecourse which has been the home of the Derby since 1780. Cyclists can use most of the tracks over Epsom and Walton Downs.

Stane Street The former Roman road from London Bridge to Chichester, it is now a bridleway from Epsom to Mickleham Downs.

Headley 15thC Cock Inn.

Betchworth An attractive village.

Brockham Has one of the prettiest village greens in Surrey.

Leigh The church contains many interesting brasses.

c The route via Charlwood is more attractive, but that via Hookwood is shorter.

Charlwood Scenic village with 11thC church and 16th and 17thC houses.

Tinsley Green Venue of the annual British Individual Marbles Championship on Good Friday.

Gatwick Airport A former RAF airfield, it is now London's second largest civil airport.

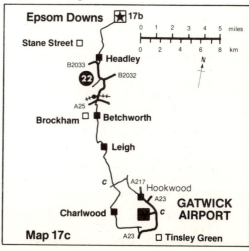

Map 17c

the A3 roundabout.

b The alternative route is more complex but passes the tennis ground and is generally less trafficked.

Wimbledon Venue for the All England Lawn Tennis Championships, started in 1877; the present courts date from 1922. John Evelyn museum.

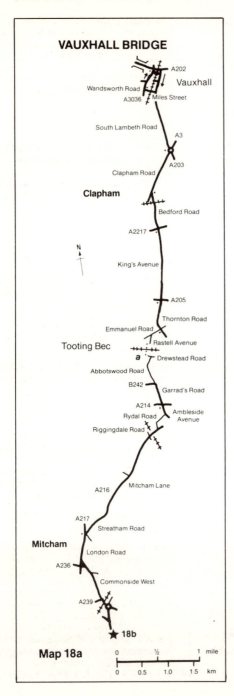

VAUXHALL BRIDGE

A202
Vauxhall
Wandsworth Road
A3036 Miles Street
South Lambeth Road
A3
A203
Clapham Road
Clapham
Bedford Road
A2217
King's Avenue
N
A205
Thornton Road
Emmanuel Road
Rastell Avenue
Tooting Bec
a Drewstead Road
Abbotswood Road
B242
Garrad's Road
A214
Rydal Road Ambleside
Avenue
Riggingdale Road
A216 Mitcham Lane
A217
Streatham Road
Mitcham
London Road
A236
Commonside West
A239
★ 18b
Map 18a
0   ½   1 mile
0   0.5   1.0   1.5 km

Route 18
**VAUXHALL BRIDGE - REIGATE &
BLETCHINGLEY
21 miles (34 km) to Reigate or
Bletchingley**

Bartholomew: 1:100,000: 9
OS 1:50,000: 176, 187

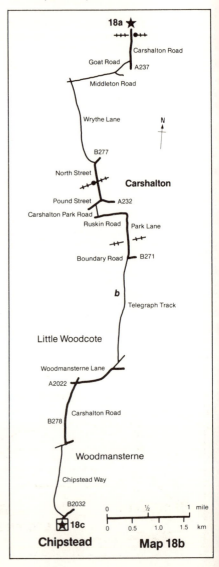

18a ★
Carshalton Road
Goat Road
A237
Middleton Road
Wrythe Lane
N
B277
North Street
Carshalton
Pound Street
A232
Carshalton Park Road
Ruskin Road Park Lane
Boundary Road B271
b
Telegraph Track
Little Woodcote
Woodmansterne Lane
A2022
Carshalton Road
B278
Woodmansterne
Chipstead Way
B2032
☆ 18c
Chipstead   **Map 18b**
0   ½   1 mile
0   0.5   1.0   1.5 km

Clapham Suburb with a fine common. Samuel Pepys died in a house by here.

a A short rough, but rideable, track under the railway avoids busy roads.

Mitcham Noted for its breezy common, which was one of the earliest homes of English golf. The lower green is famous for its cricket.

Carshalton Old village pond. Anne Boleyn's well is close to the parish church.

b Telegraph Track is a RUPP through small holdings. It is generally a smooth concrete road with entry from the north via a narrower path with posts.

c The main route uses a partly loose-stone road RUPP through the grounds of Gatton Hall School.

Reigate 18thC market house. The windmill on Reigate Heath is now used as a church.

Farthing Downs Saxon tumuli, nature trail.

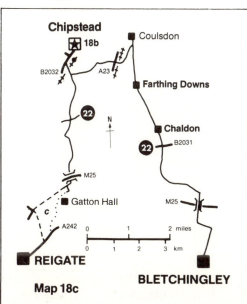

Map 18c

Chaldon 11thC church whose treasures include the oldest bell in Surrey and the most complete 12thC wall painting in England: *'The Ladder of Salvation'*.

Bletchingley Wide, picturesque main street. Norman castle remains.

Route 19
LAMBETH BRIDGE - CROCKHAM HILL & ROYAL TUNBRIDGE WELLS
27 miles (43 km) to Crockham Hill;
42 miles (67 km) to Royal Tunbridge Wells

Bartholomew: 1:100,000: 9
OS 1:50,000: 177, 187, 188 (Royal Tunbridge Wells only)

Lambeth Bridge - Sydenham: for details of places of interest en route, see Route 5.

a Dismount to use footpath under railway between Lennard Road and Park Road.

Beckenham A suburb with some character and Victorian houses. The church has a 13thC lychgate. To the south, Langley Park golf course was once the park of a large house.

West Wickham A 1920s suburb. Near the church - a restored 15thC building with its original lychgate - is the former Wickham Court, a red-bricked turreted house built in 1480 and now used as the Coloma College.

Biggin Hill The aerodrome is the venue for air shows.

Titsey The small estate village of Titsey Park. The church contains 14thC tiles. A Roman villa has been discovered to the south.

Westerham A pleasing country town with many old buildings. Quebec House (NT, open) was the home of General Wolfe and Squerries Court (sometimes open) was where he was handed his first commission. Westerham Hill is highest in Kent.

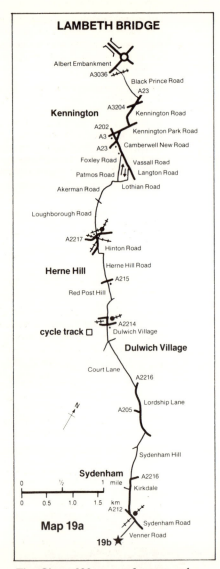

Map 19a

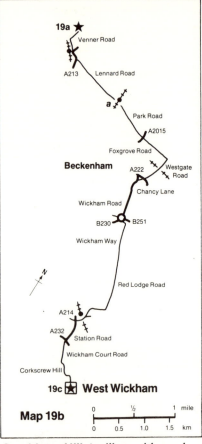

Map 19b

Crockham Hill A village with good views over the Weald. There is a cenotaph to Octavia Hill who did much to found the National Trust and who is buried in the churchyard. NT properties nearby include Chartwell (open), the former home of Sir Winston Churchill, Grange Farm and Close Farm.

The Chart 320 acres of greensand ridge in this area are owned by the NT.

Limpsfield An attractive village whose High Street includes buildings from the 15th-19thC

b The route via the bridleway is shorter, but may be muddy after wet weather.

Holwood Park Once the home of Pitt, but rebuilt by Burton in 1825. Nearby is Caesar's Camp, an ancient fort.

Downe A peaceful village, the 13thC church has a shingled spire. Down House was the home of Charles Darwin for 40 years and where he

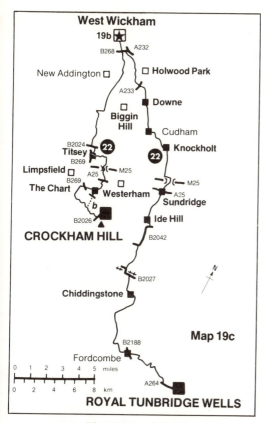

West Wickham
19b ⭐
B268   A232
New Addington ☐   ☐ Holwood Park
A233
☐   ■ Downe
Biggin
Hill
☐ Cudham
B2024   (22)
Titsey   ■ Knockholt
B269   (22)
Limpsfield ☐   M25
A25
B269   ☐   M25
The Chart   ■ A25
Westerham   ■ Sundridge
b
CROCKHAM HILL   ▲   ■ Ide Hill
B2026   B2042

N

B2027

Chiddingstone

Map 19c

B2188
Fordcombe
0 1 2 3 4 5 miles
0 2 4 6 8 km
A264 ◄
ROYAL TUNBRIDGE WELLS

wrote *The Origin of Species*. It is now owned by the Royal College of Surgeons (open).

Knockholt A village with character and pride and the highest in Kent. Knockholt Beeches to the south is a landmark for miles.

Sundridge A village with many old houses including Old Hall (NT), a 15thC timbered hall-house with a great hall and original stone hearth.

Ide Hill There are good views over the Weald from the NT viewpoint. The pleasing hamlet consists of cottages and an inn around a green.

Chiddingstone A picturesque village with 16th and 17thC timber houses and Castle Inn owned by the NT. The 14thC church has a tower with

octagonal turrets. Chiddingstone Castle is a 19thC pseudo-Gothic building which includes parts of an earlier Carolean house. It is now open as a museum.

Royal Tunbridge Wells A spa since the 17thC and 'Royal' since 1909, the town has many Regency and Victorian buildings. The Pantiles is a terraced walk with attractive shops behind a colonnade. The charming church of King Charles the Martyr was built in 1678 and has an interesting wooden cupola.

Route 20
WATERLOO BRIDGE - KEMSING
28 miles (44 km)

Bartholomew: 1:100,000: 9
OS 1:50,000: 177, 188

Bermondsey Long the centre of London's leather trade, there is a leather market in Weston Street. The area is also famous for rope-making and the distilling of vinegar.

a If you ride south it is necessary to negotiate the whole of Lower Road gyratory, or you may prefer to dismount and walk from Rotherhithe New Road to Trundleys Road.

Deptford A densely populated area, once famous for its noble dockyard.

Lewisham The Clock Tower in the High Street was erected to mark Queen Victoria's diamond jubilee. The obelisk at the foot of Lewisham Hill dates from 1866 and was originally a drinking fountain.

Lee Dr Edmund Halley, Astronomer Royal and discoverer of the comet named after him, is buried in the graveyard of the old church, opposite the present parish church of St Margaret.

Eltham College The former buildings of the Royal Naval School, opened in 1889.

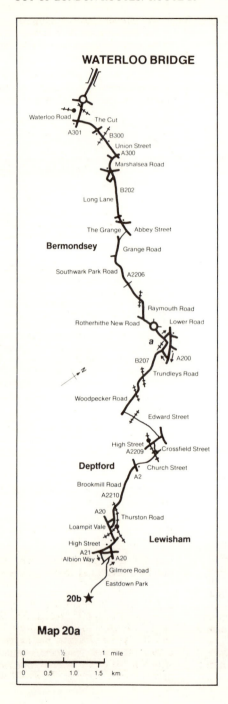

WATERLOO BRIDGE

Waterloo Road
The Cut
A301
B300
Union Street
A300
Marshalsea Road
B202
Long Lane
The Grange   Abbey Street
Bermondsey
Grange Road
Southwark Park Road   A2206
Raymouth Road
Rotherhithe New Road   Lower Road
a
B207   A200
Trundleys Road
Woodpecker Road
Edward Street
High Street   Crossfield Street
A2209
Deptford   Church Street
A2
Brookmill Road
A2210
A20   Thurston Road
Loampit Vale
High Street   **Lewisham**
A21
Albion Way   A20
Gilmore Road
Eastdown Park
20b ★

Map 20a

0   ½   1 mile
0   0.5   1.0   1.5   km

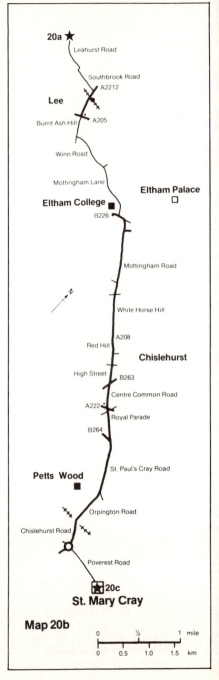

20a ★
Leahurst Road
Southbrook Road
A2212
Lee
Burnt Ash Hill   A205
Winn Road
Mottingham Lane
Eltham Palace □
Eltham College ■
B226
Mottingham Road
White Horse Hill
A208
Red Hill
Chislehurst
High Street   B263
Centre Common Road
A222
Royal Parade
B264
St. Paul's Cray Road
Petts Wood ■
Orpington Road
Chislehurst Road
Poverest Road
20c
St. Mary Cray

Map 20b

0   ½   1 mile
0   0.5   1.0   1.5   km

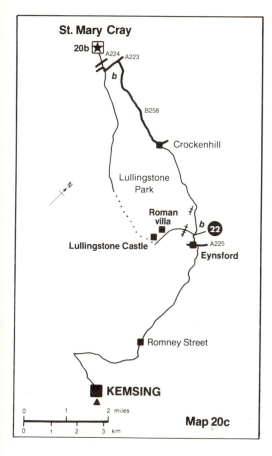

Map 20c

Petts Wood Purchased by the National Trust in 1927 as a memorial to William Willett, founder of Summer Time.

St Mary Cray An industrial area with several paper mills. The church has some rare late 18thC brasses.

b The route via Lullingstone Park is more pleasant and traffic-free, but uses a loose stone track which is not a right of way. The approaches to Eynsford from Crockenhill and Romney Street are steep.

Lullingstone Castle Actually a fortified Tudor manor house, the home of the Hart-Dyke family since about 1500. Interesting 14thC chapel of St Botolph nearby.

Lullingstone Roman Villa Dating from AD90, this Villa has one of the best preserved mosaic floors in the country. There is also a Christian chapel above. Open, DoE.

Eynsford An attractive village and popular tourist spot amidst delightful countryside. There is a hump-backed bridge and ford in front of a Tudor house and a group of half-timbered cottages. Also the ruins of a Norman castle (open, DoE).

Kemsing A village on the Pilgrim's Way. The pretty church has a 14thC timber porch.

Eltham Palace Only the banqueting hall remains of the palace where Henry VIII and Elizabeth I spent several years of their childhood. There is also a moat, crossed by a 15thC bridge. Open, DoE.

Chislehurst A 'select' suburb with a fine birch and woodland Common. Nearby is a small group of old village houses, shops and an inn. The 15thC St Nicholas church has a Bethersden marble font. To the west is Camden Place, built in 1609, home of Napoleon III in exile in the late 19thC and now a golf clubhouse. Also the famous Chislehurst Caves, the remains of a chalk mine worked since Roman times. Open.

Route 21
LONDON BRIDGE - ROCHESTER
34 miles (54 km)

Bartholomew: 1:100,000: 9, 10
OS 1:50,000: 177, 178

London Bridge - Greenwich: for details of places of interest en route, see Route 5.

a The route from London Bridge to Greenwich uses busy roads. For those with more time to spare, Route 5 shows a more pleasant, but longer, alternative route. A second alternative would be to go by train between these points (direct service). To avoid much suburban cycling, a train can be used between London Bridge and Dartford.

b The road through Greenwich Park closes at dusk (1800 winter). After this time follow the alternative route.

Carlton House A former Jacobean manor house, now used as a library and community centre.

Woolwich A town with military connections. Woolwich Arsenal is still used for the design and manufacture of armaments and the Royal Artillery Barracks are at Woolwich Common. On the west side of the Common, the Rotunda, a circular building almost 40yds across, was designed by Nash and now houses an interesting artillery museum. There is a free ferry across the Thames to North Woolwich.

Castle Wood (Shooter's Hill Park) A park of 22 acres with a beautiful terrace garden giving views over the London suburbs and the Surrey Hills. Above is Severndroog Castle, a triangular tower built in 1784 in honour of Sir William James and named after the Malabar coast pirate stronghold he took in 1775.

Plumstead Common An open space acquired for the public in 1877-78. From Bostall Heath, nearby, there are fine views over the Thames.

Lesnes Abbey Founded in 1178 by Richard de Lucy, only ruins now remain. The site is open as a public park.

Bexleyheath At Upton, east of Danson Park, is the Red House: a brick and tile Victorian villa designed by Philip Webb for William Morris in 1859.

Crayford An industrial area, the church, 15thC, includes lovely monuments to William Draper and Elizabeth Shovel.

Dartford The priory in Victoria Road and now used as offices, is the remains of a Dominican nunnery founded in 1349. The Bull Hotel in the High Street has a galleried Georgian yard, roofed over. Holy Trinity Church, 13thC,

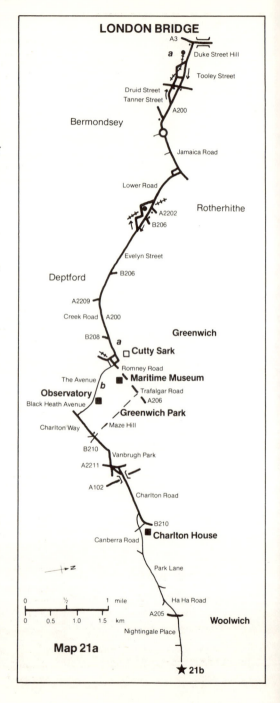

LONDON BRIDGE

A3
a — Duke Street Hill
Tooley Street
Druid Street
Tanner Street
A200

Bermondsey

Jamaica Road

Lower Road

Rotherhithe
A2202
B206

Evelyn Street

Deptford   B206

A2209
Creek Road   A200

B208   *a*
Greenwich
□ Cutty Sark
Romney Road
The Avenue   *b*   ■ Maritime Museum
Observatory   Trafalgar Road
Black Heath Avenue   ■   A206
                    Greenwich Park
Charlton Way   Maze Hill

B210   Vanbrugh Park
A2211

A102   Charlton Road

B210
Canberra Road   ■ Charlton House

Park Lane

Ha Ha Road
A205   Woolwich
Nightingale Place

Map 21a

★ **21b**

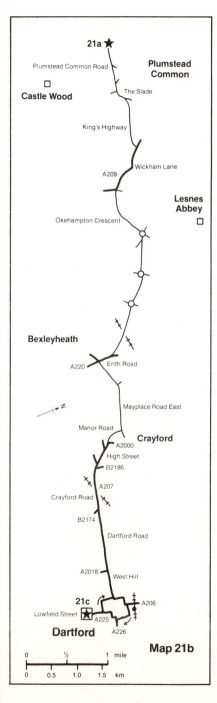

includes a 15thC wall painting.
Dartford, founded where Watling
Street crossed the River Darent, has
long been a papermaking centre and
modern industries also include flour
mills, chemical works, shipbuilding and
cement. Wat Tyler lived here as did
Applegarth, the inventor of rotary
printing.

Sutton-at-Hone St John's Jerusalem
includes the remains of the 13thC
Commandery of the Knights
Hospitallers, at which Henry III often
stayed. There is also a large garden,
which is open on Wednesday
afternoons from April to October. NT.

Darenth An old village with a green
and Saxon church beside the River
Darent, surrounded by new
development.

Meopham A village of cottages and
inns with typical Kentish facades and a
church tower which is visible for miles.
To the south, Meopham Green has a
famous cricket green and also a well
preserved smock mill.

Luddesdown A small village in
forested and hilly country.
Luddesdown Court is an early manor
house including examples of Saxon,
Norman and Tudor work. It is thought
to be the oldest continuously inhabited
house in Britain. At Dode, near Great
Buckland, are the remains of a village
abandoned after the Black Death.

Cobham The church is famous for its
monuments, especially brasses. The
'Leathern Bottle Inn' is associated with
Charles Dickens. Cobham Hall (DoE,
NT) is a Jacobean house in grounds by
Repton and Owletts (NT, open W and
Th afternoons in summer) a redbrick
house of Charles II's reign with
cottages, garden and orchards.

Cuxton An industrial village with good
views over the Medway.

*c The route crosses the Medway via a
cycle path alongside the M4. From the
west turn just north of the bridge onto
a path signed 'Cycle track to Borstal'.
A similar sign to Cuxton and Strood
shows the route from the east.*

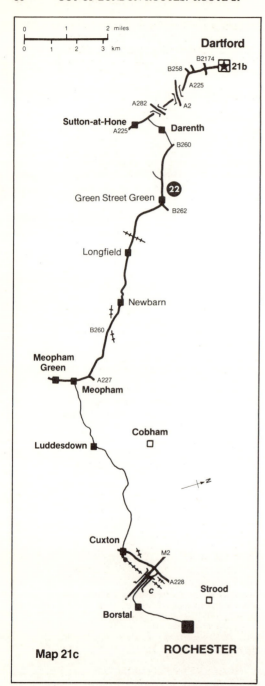

Map 21c

Borstal Fort Borstal was one of a chain of fortresses built as part of the Medway defences against Napoleon. It has since given its name to the penal institution which now occupies the site.

Strood An urban area combined with Rochester since 1836. Temple Manor (DoE), a 13thC manor, has recently been restored.

Rochester An ancient and historic cathedral city. Of the castle only the Norman keep (DoE, open) survives, but this is one of the best castellated ruins in the country. Built in 1130 and largely intact, there are good views from the battlements. Bridge Chapel, near Cubitt's iron bridge, was originally built in 1397 for pilgrims and other travellers. Nearby are remains of the old town wall. The Guildhall, 1687, is supported on coupled Doric columns and is topped by a copper weather vane, 5 ft high, of a full-rigged ship. The cathedral is more interesting than beautiful, including a jumble of styles and periods. The crypt is one of the largest and finest in England and contains some 13thC graffiti. Rochester has many old inns including the Bull Hotel, an old coaching inn depicted in Dickens' *Great Expectations* and *Pickwick Papers* . Eastgate House, 1590, is now a museum and contains in its grounds Dickens' chalet from Gadhill, where he wrote many of his works.

Route 22
LONDON ORBITAL ROUTE
150 miles (240 km) - round trip

Bartholomew: 1:100,000: 9, 10, 15, 16
OS: 1:50,000: 166, 167, 176, 177, 187, 188

This route is intended to be used in three different ways. The sporting cyclist might like the challenge of riding its entire length in one day, knowing that if he has to give up a train back to central London will never be far away. The not so energetic cyclist can use the orbital route to link together radial routes, using one such route for the outward journey and another for the return. The cyclist with more limited horizons, who wishes to ride only a few miles in the country without travelling too far from London, can use a train to and from stations near the orbital route.

Generally, the route keeps to minor roads away from built up areas, but some use of classified roads and roads through towns is unavoidable, particularly in south-west London.

Description anti-clockwise from Tilbury to Gravesend

a Cycles are carried on the regular passenger ferry service linking Gravesend with Tilbury Riverside.

Tilbury A busy port, both passenger and commercial, and a major container transhipment dock. Tilbury Fort, near the ferry, has a gatehouse of 1682 and the church includes the earliest Norman work in England.

Chadwell St Mary Sleepers Farm is a charming timber-framed house, complete with thatched roof. Much of the original 15thC woodwork is intact although the door is 17thC. The church nearby has an interesting parapet with brick and flint chequerwork. There is an early 18thC carved chair in the chancel.

Orsett An attractive village with timbered houses, some overhanging. The church which dates from 1160 has two sun dials by the doorway.

Bulphan A village only six feet above sea level in the middle of flat country. There are interesting 15thC and 16thC buildings, including Appleton's Farm, which upper storey overhangs both wings of a hall. By the green is an old barn and a lychgate.

Brentwood The Big School is the survivor of the original buildings of the public school, founded in 1557 by Sir Anthony Browne. The town has a wide main street, fine old houses and attractive inns.

South Weald Attractive old houses and inns of various periods and the church includes mediaeval glass in its tower. Buried here is Lord Chief Justice Scroggs, responsible for the prosecutions in the bogus Papish plot of Titus Oates.

Navestock see Route 6.

Theydon Bois Old cottages around an attractive village green. The church has a window to the memory of Frances May Buss, founder of the North London Collegiate School, who revolutionized teaching methods.

Loughton The home of Thomas Willingale, who successfully fought in the 19thC for Epping Forest to remain public property.

Epping Forest see Route 7

Waltham Abbey, Waltham Cross see Route 8.

Potters Bar A residential satellite town. To the south Wrotham Hall was built in 1754 by Isaac Ware for Admiral Byng and is of pure Burlingtonian-Palladian design. Further west the house at Dyrham Park has a detached portico of Tuscan columns and a monumental gateway to the north-east. At Knightsland Farm there is a farmhouse with 16thC wall paintings telling the story of the Prodigal Sun.

Shenley see Route 10.

b The alternative route uses a bridleway from London Colney to

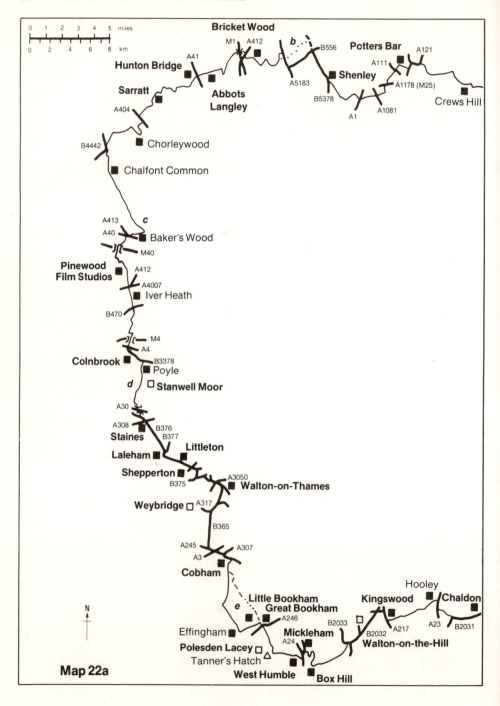

Map 22a

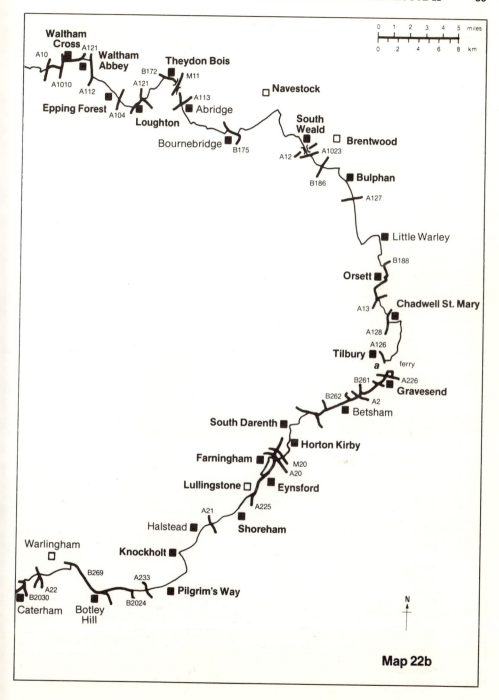

Map 22b

Colney Street and then another west of the A5183 to the Bricket Wood road. These can be muddy after wet weather.

Bricket Wood A residential suburb of Watford surrounded by woodlands. The Building Research Station is here.

Abbots Langley The birthplace of the only Englishman to become Pope. Nicholas Breakspear, the son of a poor man, was left to his own resources at St Albans monastery but went on to become Pope Hadrian IV. St Lawrence's church is of architectural interest with a 13thC low west tower with diagonal buttresses. It houses many monuments.

Hunton Bridge See Route 23.

Sarratt A pretty village with a long green and 17thC farmhouses. The church tower has an unusual saddleback roof and there are pre Victorian almshouses opposite.

c The road linking Higher Denham with the A40 is a RUPP with a stony surface. It is easily rideable although flooding sometimes occurs where it crosses the River Misbourne. It is approached from the south via a service road which leaves the A40 at its junction with the A413.

Pinewood Film Studios see Route 13.

Colnbrook see Route 14

d Moor Lane, which forms part of the route, is to be closed for construction of the M25. A replacement bridleway, specially designed for use by cyclists and with an all-weather surface, is to be provided on the east side of the motorway.

Stanwell Moor A mediaeval village. The church includes a monument to Lord Kayvett, who arrested Guy Fawkes, and his Lady.

Staines A town to which access is now difficult for cyclists because of the construction of new roads. The most interesting buildings are around Church Street and High Street. The London Stone, in the park west of the church, dates from 1285 and marked the limit of jurisdiction of the City of London over the River Thames. It is still the boundary between the Upper and Lower Thames.

Laleham There are Georgian and neo-Georgian houses around a pleasant green and the church includes two 12thC arcades. South of the village is a particularly pleasant open stretch of the Thames.

Littleton A hamlet of timber-framed cottages. The church is part of the former village school. Shepperton Film Studios are here.

Shepperton see Route 15.

Walton-on-Thames Fine 15thC Old Manor House, once the home of John Bradshaw. Also many good modern buildings. The church of St Mary has many fine monuments and brasses.

Weybridge Oatlands Park was the site of a palace built in 1588 for Henry VIII.

Cobham see Route 16.

e The alternative route is quieter but makes use of a bridleway over Great Bookham Common.

Little Bookham The 12thC church is the remains of a much larger Norman building. There is a small belfry and an interesting tub font bound with iron straps.

Great Bookham St Nicholas's church has a weatherboarded west tower and a shingled spire. The Hermitage, formerly Fairfield House, was where Fanny Burney wrote *Camilla.*

Polesden Lacy The house was built by Thomas Cubitt in 1824 and extended in 1906. It contains the Greville collection of fine paintings, tapestries, furniture and china. NT, open on most afternoons in summer.

West Humble Originally only a few houses, but expanded into a dormitory suburb in the 1930s. There are remains of a 12thC chapel (NT), built for those unable to cross the river to Mickleham church.

Mickleham A picture postcard village with a genial church, amidst lovely scenery. Lord Nelson stayed at the Burford Bridge Hotel just before Trafalgar. Juniper Hall (NT) is a fine house at the foot of Little Switzerland Valley.

Box Hill A sublime viewpoint with views over the Weald, South Downs, Mickleham Valley and Ranmore, but often very crowded. The hill is named after the profusion of box trees which cling to the precipitous slopes. The climb from the west is the nearest approach to an Alpine road in southern England, complete with hairpin bends.

Walton-on-the-Hill A mere pond, a green and a golf course.

Kingswood St Andrew's church is a 19thC copy of 14thC church at Shottesbrooke in Berkshire.

Chaldon see Route 18.

Pilgrim's Way A pre-Roman route from the Cornish tin mines to Dover. It may have been used by pilgrims to Canterbury after the murder of Thomas à Becket, but it only received its name in the 19thC.

Knockholt see Route 19.

Shoreham A quiet but attractive village with many willows alongside the River Darent. The cross carved in the chalk above the village is a 1914-18 war memorial.

Lullingstone, Eynsford see Route 20.

Farningham A charming village astride the Darent. There is a picturesque water flour mill together with a rich miller's house. Also several early large houses.

Horton Kirby Predominantly neo-Elizabethan buildings.

South Darenth Papermills and an imposing railway viaduct.

Gravesend This is a nautical and an industrial town, with a famous yachting centre, the pilot station of the Port of London Authority and the National Sea Training School of the Merchant Service. The church of St Andrew has a memorial to the ill-fated Arctic expedition of 1845, led by Sir John Franklin and St George's church (1731) is on the site of a former church where Red Indian Princess Pocohontas was buried in 1617. The Princess played an important part in the settlement of Virginia and the church is a place of pilgrimage for Americans.

6. TOWPATH CYCLING

London seen from its canal and river towpaths is a completely different world where much has remained unchanged for many decades and a bicycle is a good way of exploring it.

Towpaths differ in many respects from other routes for cyclists. It is possible to ride them throughout without meeting a motor vehicle, stopping at a traffic light or climbing a steep hill. Indeed, but for a few tunnels en route, it is possible to continue in similar manner along the Grand Union Canal towpath for 168 miles to Langley Mill in Derbyshire or, via other canals, to places as far away as Gargrave in North Yorkshire.

Although the towpaths in London are generally easy to ride, they are certainly not race tracks and speeds will usually need to be lower than those used on the roads. However, away from the rush and bustle of other traffic, this pace will seem both natural and desirable, engendering a saner way of living. Despite this, however, for some journeys towpaths can still offer the quickest routes between parts of London and in this way they can be very valuable to the commuter.

Canals

Cyclists do not have a right to cycle on canal towpaths, but are permitted to do so if they purchase a towpath cycling permit from the British Waterways Board (BWB). These permits cost £1 per calendar year, yet the rewards of being able to use these peaceful routes are worth far more. Issued partly to relieve the BWB of responsibility in the event of an accident - the holder must sign an indemnity before it is valid - the permits cover most of the canals in Britain for which the BWB is responsible. They can be obtained from: The Estate Officer, British Waterways Board, Willow Grange, Church Road, Watford Herts, WD1 3QA.

In addition to the Grand Union Canal and Lea Navigation described in this book, cyclists with permits may also use the Regent's Canal between Islington and Limehouse and the Limehouse Cut between Limehouse and Bow. In several places in Inner London the boroughs and the Greater London Council are developing attractive Canal Way Parks along the towpaths and notices proclaim 'No Cycling'. These restrictions do *not* apply to holders of BWB permits although some officials may not be aware of this as the exemption is only referred to indirectly in the displayed bye-laws.

Rivers

Generally cycling is only permitted along river towpaths where these coincide with bridleway rights of way. However, an important exception is along the Thames towpath upstream from Teddington lock. Here the Thames Water Authority permits cycling, without permit, subject only to local restrictions imposed by private landowners. These are few. Theoretically cyclists can ride all the way along the Thames from Teddington to beyond Oxford, except that in a few places the towpath changes banks without a bridge or ferry!

Down Thames from Teddington the Port of London Authority has jurisdiction for the towpath and cycling is mostly prohibited.

Riding technique

Because towpath cycling is so different from riding along the roads, some special notes concerning riding technique are desirable, with particular reference to the Grand Union Canal and Lea Navigation.

Although there is no motor traffic with which to contend, towpath cycling still requires great care and attention. The most obvious danger, of ending up in the water, is not very great along the towpaths within Greater London. Nearly everywhere the towpaths are wide: 2 - 3 yards being the average along the Grand Union, wider still along the Lea and the Thames. Often there is a grass verge along the water edge and this, together with the fact that the water is nearly level with the banks and not some distance below, gives a greater feeling of stability.

The surfaces of towpaths are as variable as the scenery through which they pass. Variable too from year to year as well as from place to place. Generally in the London area the surfaces are good, being of fine stone in the suburbs and ash or tarmac further in. The Grand Union Canal from Acton to Paddington and the Regent's Canal on to Victoria Park has a particularly good surface: CEGB concrete cable ducts. However, short sections of poorer surface will be found in many places and cyclists should be particularly careful where there are newly laid deep stones.

Unfortunately the worst hazards occur where they cannot easily be seen: under bridges. Every bridge should be approached with caution. Along the Grand Union in particular the path is often dark, wet and badly potholed and sometimes cross-ribbing is provided. Many of the older hump-backed bridges also have only a narrow towpath beneath with a sharp bend on either side and restricted headroom. Adjacent to locks the approach is also sometimes steep with loose stones. It is advisable to dismount for these short stretches.

Another bridge hazard affects underbridges as well as overbridges. The towpath on or under the bridge is usually brick or concrete; the ground to either side is earth covered with fine gravel or a similar material. Needless to say erosion affects the latter more than the former resulting in a high kerb at the bridge edge. Once more, take care.

Although there are no steep hills along a canal, there are nevertheless some very steep underbridges. These occur where the towpath either changes sides or crosses a side arm of the canal. Being mostly original canal furniture, these are hump-backed with very steep sides and a short top. Unless you have very low gears, these must be walked. They are also often ribbed. This helped the horses but stops a cyclist.

Although towpaths generally drain well, there often remain some puddles and a few waterlogged sections. Usually the water here is not deep, but the possibility of potholes beneath should not be overlooked.

Apart from the natural hazards there are also human ones. Many sections of the waterways abound with fishermen whose rods and tackle are often strewn across the path. There are also many people out for a stroll. All these people enjoy the towpaths for their peace and tranquility and a bicycle does little to disturb this. Therefore, often people will be unaware of the approach of a cycle behind them. A hurried approach, sharp braking or a close pass could surprise them and will do nothing for the reputation of cyclists in general; nor is this the place to ring a bell or sound a horn. A slow approach followed by a polite 'excuse me' is just as effective and far better received.

Lest the foregoing sounds discouraging, it must be said that the majority of the towpath routes offer easy and pleasant cycling. Although there are a few places in the outer suburbs where a very low gear is necessary to keep moving, most of the routes can be ridden comfortably with a gear around 65 inches. It is best, however, to keep to a gear lower than that so as to be ready for different conditions which can occur quite suddenly.

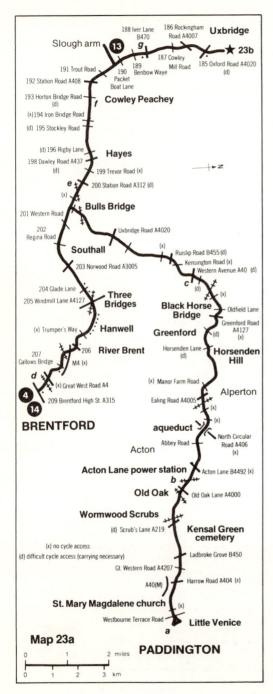

Map 23a

- Slough arm
- **13**
- 188 Iver Lane B470
- 186 Rockingham Road A4007
- **Uxbridge**
- *g*
- ★ **23b**
- 187 Cowley Mill Road
- 185 Oxford Road A4020 (d)
- 191 Trout Road
- 190 Packet Boat Lane
- 189 Benbow Waye
- 192 Station Road A408
- 193 Horton Bridge Road (d)
- *f*
- **Cowley Peachey**
- (x) 194 Iron Bridge Road
- (d) 195 Stockley Road
- (d) 196 Rigby Lane
- **Hayes**
- 198 Dawley Road A437 (d)
- 199 Trevor Road (x)
- 200 Station Road A312 (d)
- *e*
- (x)
- **Bulls Bridge**
- 201 Western Road
- 202 Regina Road
- Uxbridge Road A4020
- **Southall**
- (x)
- Ruislip Road B455 (d)
- 203 Norwood Road A3005
- Kensington Road (x)
- Western Avenue A40 (d)
- 204 Glade Lane
- 205 Windmill Lane A4127
- **Three Bridges**
- *c*
- (d)
- (x)
- **Black Horse Bridge**
- Oldfield Lane
- Greenford Road A4127 (x)
- (x) Trumper's Way
- **Hanwell**
- **Greenford**
- (d)
- Horsenden Lane (d)
- **Horsenden Hill**
- 207 Gallows Bridge
- 206
- **River Brent**
- M4 (x)
- *d*
- (x) Manor Farm Road
- **Alperton**
- **4**
- **14**
- (x) Great West Road A4
- 209 Brentford High St. A315
- Ealing Road A4005
- (x)
- **BRENTFORD**
- **aqueduct**
- (x)
- North Circular Road A406 (x)
- **Acton**
- Abbey Road
- **Acton Lane power station**
- *b*
- Acton Lane B4492 (x)
- **Old Oak**
- Old Oak Lane A4000
- **Wormwood Scrubs**
- (d) Scrub's Lane A219
- **Kensal Green cemetery**
- (x) no cycle access
- (d) difficult cycle access (carrying necessary)
- Ladbroke Grove B450
- Gt. Western Road A4207
- A40(M)
- Harrow Road A404 (x)
- **St. Mary Magdalene church**
- (x)
- Westbourne Terrace Road
- **Little Venice**
- *a*
- 0   1   2 miles
- 0   1   2   3 km
- **PADDINGTON**

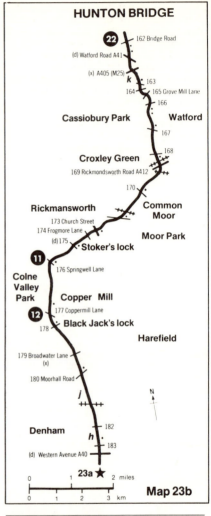

Map 23b

- **HUNTON BRIDGE**
- **22**
- 162 Bridge Road
- (d) Watford Road A41
- (x) A405 (M25)
- *k*
- 163
- 164
- 165 Grove Mill Lane
- 166
- **Cassiobury Park**
- **Watford**
- 167
- 168
- **Croxley Green**
- 169 Rickmansworth Road A412
- 170
- **Rickmansworth**
- **Common Moor**
- 173 Church Street
- 174 Frogmore Lane
- **Moor Park**
- (d) 175
- **Stoker's lock**
- **11**
- 176 Springwell Lane
- **Colne Valley Park**
- **Copper Mill**
- 177 Coppermill Lane
- **12**
- 178
- **Black Jack's lock**
- **Harefield**
- 179 Broadwater Lane (x)
- 180 Moorhall Road
- *j*
- N
- **Denham**
- 182
- *h*
- 183
- (d) Western Avenue A40
- **23a** ★
- 0   1   2 miles
- 0   1   2   3 km

Route 23

PADDINGTON AND BRENTFORD - HUNTON BRIDGE VIA THE GRAND UNION CANAL
**31 miles (50 km) from Paddington;
24 miles (38 km) from Brentford**

Bartholomew: 1:100,000: 9, 15
OS 1:50,000: 176. Also 166 for last ½ mile.

Bridge numbers: It is sometimes difficult to know exactly where you have reached along a canal because progress is slower and the surroundings so unfamiliar. Along the Grand Union 'main line' from Brentford this is aided by small oval number plates fixed to the crests of most bridges. These numbers are reproduced on the accompanying maps. This system was not adopted along the branch from Paddington.

Little Venice Also known as 'Paddington Stop' by boatmen, this junction between the Grand Union and Regent's Canals is a picturesque area surrounded by Regency houses. Waterborne shows are sometimes held here.

a Normal access to the towpath is down the slope from Warwick Crescent near Westbourne Terrace Road. However, sometimes gates here or further along the towpath past the mooring area are closed, then access should be gained through the park at the end of Delamere Terrace.

St Mary Magdalene Church Built 1868-78, the crypt is richly decorated.

Kensal Green cemetery The resting place of many famous people including Trollope, Thackeray, Leigh Hunt and Blondin. Coffins were at one time able to arrive by canal and the former water gates in the cemetery wall can still be seen.

Wormwood Scrubs A large expanse of open space with many football pitches. The famous prison is the dominant building on the far side. Cyclists may use the path just north of the prison, which is the only one to cross the Scrubs.

Old Oak An area riddled with railway tracks linking the London Midland and Western Region main lines. There is an important locomotive and carriage depot south of the canal.

Acton Lane power station This straddles the canal. Here ends the immaculate paved towpath surface provided by the ducts of the CEGB cables which are routed along the Grand Union, Regent's and Hertford

Union canals and the Northern Outfall Sewer to Beckton in east London.

b Through the power station the towpath is narrow and the surface poor but it is much improved thereafter.

North Circular Road aqueduct For cyclists, this is the safest and most peaceful crossing of this notorious road.

Horsenden Hill A wood and public park. The bridleway around the east side provides some good rough-stuff cycling.

Greenford A residential area. South from here the canal has a very rural setting although this will change when the new industrial estate on the opposite bank is completed. There are a number of disused side-arms around here, which the towpath crosses by steep-sided bridges.

Black Horse Bridge: The canal makes a wide U-turn here and then heads south-west. There are a number of disused private wharves in this area.

c The towpath beneath the A40 Western Avenue bridge is ribbed and particularly hazardous for cycling. Slow down to a crawl or dismount.

Brentford A busy canal depot, still handling some commercial traffic. Boats queue here to await the opening, near high tide, of the locks into the Thames.

d Just north of the locks the towpath 'disappears' inside a large modern warehouse, of which it skirts two sides. Eventually it re-emerges to a beautiful stretch, marred only by the closeness of the M4 motorway.

River Brent This river joins the canal south of Hanwell locks and the towpath crosses a number of weirs where the river course subsequently meanders from the canal.

Hanwell Locks A steep hill, by canal standards, seven locks in tandem raise the canal by 53 feet. A very picturesque area.

Three Bridges At one point a road (Windmill Lane) crosses the canal which in turn crosses a railway line. This rare example of a triple bridge is a protected national monument and is best viewed from the road.

Southall An area with a large Asian community, reflected in the wide range of shops in the extensive shopping centre. Southall Library (Osterley Park Road) houses the Martinware pottery collection (closed Sundays).

Bulls Bridge Junction The junction between the Grand Union 'main line' and the Paddington branch. A large BWB depot is situated here.

e The towpath surface beneath the railway bridge is dark and very humpy. Take care.

Hayes An industrial suburb, contrasting in character with the more rural atmosphere in its twinned neighbour Harlington (see Route 14). There is an interesting local history museum in Golden Crescent (closed Wed afternoons and Sundays).

f A signed cycle route to Uxbridge crosses this bridge.

Cowley Peachey The branch to Slough leaves the main line at Cowley Peachey Junction. Further north, Cowley Lock marks the end of a 27-mile long pound without locks stretching to Slough, Hanwell and Camden Town. See also Route 13.

g The towpath changes sides via Iver Lane. Be careful as a cyclist turning right from this road cannot be seen too well by approaching traffic.

Uxbridge On the outskirts of suburban London, Uxbridge has a modern shopping centre and is the administrative centre for the Borough of Hillingdon. The Battle of Britain was directed from the nearby RAF station. Uxbridge lock is particularly attractive, complete with a lock cottage, a turnover bridge and a modern mill.

h Use either bridge 182 or 183 to change sides as there is a towpath between on both sides of the canal. The path on the western bank is less rough but is often crossed by mooring ropes from boats berthed there.

Denham Denham Court and Denham Place nearby are fine buildings and the village church, surrounded by cottages, contains a 15thC Dom painting and Renaissance monuments.

j The towpath surface in this area is very difficult to ride and in places the canal has made in-roads into the path. It is probably best to use roads between Uxbridge and Denham Green, but this should be done via the B467 (Harefield Road), not the A4020 which meets the A40 at a very dangerous roundabout.

Harefield see Route 11.

Black Jack's lock A timbered cottage and a small mill make a superb setting for this lock.

Copper Mill lock Adjacent is a large mill, once used for processing paper but latterly for making copper sheet for boat building. The towpath north to Springwell Lock is one of the most attractive sections.

Colne Valley Park The whole of the Colne valley from Poyle to Rickmansworth is being developed as a linear park with the emphasis on waterborne activities. The lakes around Rickmansworth have already been turned into an aquadrome catering for all kinds of water sport. Extensive footpaths and some cycle paths are also planned.

Stoker's lock Just north of the Greater London boundary. There are 16thC farm buildings nearby.

Rickmansworth A commuter suburb. Near the parish church are The Bury, 17thC, and the timber-framed Priory.

Moor Park mansion house A fine Palladian house, reconstructed in the 18thC by Sir James Thornhill and Giacomo Leoni. Thornhill, with Verrio, also provided the rich interior decoration. Open Monday afternoons (but not Bank Holidays) and other times by appointment.

Common Moor A large barren area, terminating in the north at a large paper mill which produces the famous Croxley Script.

Croxley Green Much of the large green, surrounded by old houses, survives on top of the hill. There is also a large mediaeval barn.

Watford A large town previously important for agriculture but now known for its printing industries. The centre of the town has been ruined by extensive ring roads which are hazardous and discouraging to cyclists.

Cassiobury Park A large open and wooded park, originally part of the estate of the Earls of Essex. Many of the trees in the Avenue of Limes are more than 300 years old. The park includes a nature trail, paddling pools and a miniature railway. At Grove Mill there is a water mill at a double bend on the canal and just north of this is the famous ornamental stone bridge (No.164) which the canal company were obliged to build as a condition of being allowed to pass through the Earl of Essex's estate. The canal is very picturesque in this area with the towpath twice changing sides via steep-sided accomodation bridges.

k The towpath is not continuous under the new A405/M25 bridge and walking is necessary. Despite this, the canal provides the safest way for cyclists to pass the difficult junction above.

Hunton Bridge A pretty village, now abutting King's Langley. Langleybury Park is nearby.

Continuing north: The Grand Union Canal continues north via Hemel Hempstead, Berkhamsted and Tring. The towpath is easy to ride to beyond Marsworth and the route provides an attractive and pleasant alternative to a long and busy section of the A41.

Route 24:
BOW - BROXBOURNE ALONG THE LEA NAVIGATION
18 miles (28 km)

Bartholomew: 1:100,000: 15
OS 1:50,000: 166, 177.

The River Lea (or Lee) has been an important route for trade since Roman times and the present Lea Navigation is the culmination of successive attempts to speed up traffic. Unlike the Grand Union Canal, this waterway can be used by wide lighters as well as narrow boats. Almost everywhere, cycling is easy along a wide, well surfaced path.

Bow Locks These control entry into the Lea from Bow Creek, a tidal tributary of the River Thames which is navigable only around high tide.

Three Mills, Abbey Mills pumping station: see Route 2.

Hackney Marshes: see Route 2.

Springfield Marina, Copper Mill: see Route 7.

Walthamstow Reservoirs The first of a long chain of reservoirs bordering the Lea which make an important contribution to London's water supply. They are also nature reserves being particularly rich in bird life. Large heronries exist on islands in two of the reservoirs. Generally, access is limited to birdwatchers and fishermen but Banbury reservoir is also used for yachting.

Edmonton An important centre for furniture making and a number of furniture factories border the navigation. Most of the timber used still arrives by water.

Lea Valley Regional Park A very long linear park which is being developed between Hackney Wick and Ware. Facilities for all kinds of sport are planned as well as social centres and cultural activities. Near Pickett's Lock is a large indoor leisure and sports centre as well as a new golf course.

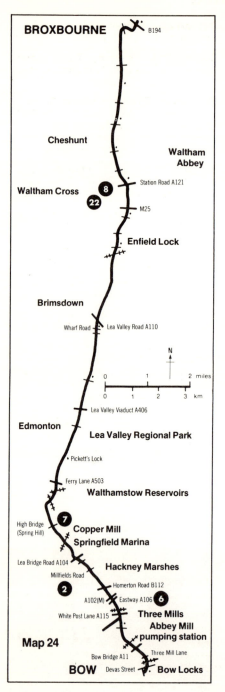

Brimsdown The BWB has opened new warehouses here in recent years: a sign of the thriving canal trade which still plies in this area.

Enfield Lock Nearby is the Royal Small Arms factory which was the birthplace of the famous Lee-Enfield rifle. Nowadays only the servicing and testing of weapons takes place.

Waltham Cross, Waltham Abbey: see Route 8.

Cheshunt In this area the navigation passes through a large expanse of wasteland although some of the flooded gravel pits are now being developed for sailing and fishing. Fishing along the Lea itself is particularly good in this area. See also Route 9.

Broxbourne The High Street contains a number of 17thC Georgian timber-framed houses and the interesting church, together with its priest's house and giant yew, date from the 15thC. Inside is an arcaded 14thC chest almost six feet long.

Continuing north: The Lea towpath can be followed through St Margarets and Ware to Hertford. At Rye House the Stort Navigation joins the Lea and this can be followed to Roydon, Harlow, Sawbridgeworth and Bishop's Stortford.

7 CROSSING THE THAMES

As well as the road bridges upriver from Tower Bridge, which are open to all traffic, there are a number of other ways of crossing the River Thames, most of which can be used by cyclists. In order from the sea these are:

Tilbury - Gravesend: passenger and cycle ferry; expensive, cycles half fare.

Dartford Tunnel: Riding through is not permitted but cycles are conveyed in a motor-towed trailer at frequent intervals. The tunnel is approached from the south by cycle track from the A226 (The Brent) adjacent to Brentfield Road and the A282 underbridge and also from Littlebrook Manor Way near Cavell Crescent (grid ref. TQ557752). On the north bank a cycle track runs to the roundabout on the A13 but cyclists are recommended to use the steps down to the A126, which is a much safer route.

North Woolwich - Woolwich: Free ferry at frequent intervals. Also cycles may be wheeled through the adjacent pedestrian tunnel which is always open (lift during day and evening).

Blackwall Tunnels: cycles prohibited.

Greenwich - Isle of Dogs: Cycles may be wheeled through the pedestrian tunnel. This is always open and a lift operates during the day and evening.

Rotherhithe Tunnel: cycling permitted.

Rotherhithe - Wapping: East London railway line, London Transport. Cycles carried out of peak hours.

Hungerford Bridge, Charing Cross — Waterloo: Cycles could be wheeled across this footbridge but as it is narrow and approached by steps it is preferable to use Waterloo Bridge.

Putney Footbridge, Ranelagh Gardens - Deodar Road: Cycles may be wheeled across; steps at either end.

Barnes Footbridge: Cycles may be wheeled across; steps either end.

Teddington Lock: Cycles may be wheeled across the footbridge which has steps at the northern end. Approach from the north by a cycle path from Riverside Drive.

Windsor: The bridge to Eton has been closed to motors but may still be used by cyclists.

Maidenhead M4 Bridge: There is a cycle path on both sides of this bridge. From Bray, take 'No Through Road' to Monkey Island, turning left just before motorway. From east use Old Dorney Lane which starts a quarter of of mile north of the motorway.

There are also a number of occasional ferries which may be able to carry cycles.

8 CYCLING IN LONDON PARKS

Although cycling is normally prohibited in parks away from motor roads, the following parks and other open spaces have paths and closed roads which have been designated as cycle routes:

Alexandra Park: the old Racecourse Road from Hornsey Gate to just inside Wood Gate and its spur to the main park road. Also the closed road from Duke's Avenue into the park.

Battersea Park: All closed roads.

Dulwich Park: The closed road from near College Road to Court Lane.

Duke's Meadows: RUPP around the perimeter.

Eltham Park: Path through Shepherdleas Wood from Eltham Park Gardens to Falconwood Station.

Epping Forest: Cyclists may use all paths.

Finsbury Park: All closed roads.

Hackney Main Marsh: The perimeter path.

Hainault Forest: All main paths, although many are sandy.

Hampstead Heath: Sandy Road from West Heath Road to North End Way. Path from opposite Downshire Hill going between second and third Hampstead Ponds (from south), by Viaduct Pond to Vale of Health and Spaniard's Road. Path from Hampstead Ponds to Millfield Lane, going between second and third Highgate Ponds. Also path from Nassington Road to Highgate Road before 1000 hrs only. (See Map 3a).

Highbury Fields: Church Path from Highbury Place to Highbury Hill.

Holland Park: Path from Ilchester Place to Duchess of Bedford's Walk and Holland Walk to Kensington High Street.

Hyde Park: Serpentine Road. Cycle paths along Broad Walk and Rotten Row. Also spur to Albert Gate.

Jackwood and Oxleas Wood: Crownwoods Lane from Kenilworth Gardens to Welling Way. Staff yard to Rochester Way near Crookston Road. Horse Ride from Crownwoods Lane to Shooters Hill.

Kensington Gardens: Closed road past Albert Memorial.

Osterley Park: Bridleway from Syon Lane to Osterley Lane.

Richmond Park: All closed roads. Also cycle path from Roehampton Gate to Richmond Gate.

Syon Park: RUPP from Brentford to Park Road.

Tooting Bec Common: Path from Doctor Johnson Avenue to Emmanuel Road at west side of Common. also path from Rastell Avenue to Drewstead Road.

Trent Park: Closed road to the staff yard.

Victoria Park: All closed roads.

Wimbledon Common: Cycle route from Kingston Road, near Roehampton Lane, to the windmill. Also Windmill Road and various bridlepaths to the south.

Wormwood Scrubs: Path from Braybrook Street to Scrubs Lane, passing back of prison and stadium.

9 CYCLES BY TRAIN

Railways provide an ideal complementary means of transport for cyclists and enables good cycling areas in the countryside to be reached easily without the need for long rides out and back through London's suburbs. The train also enables exploration of areas further afield which would be difficult or impossible to reach in a suitable time by cycling all the way.

Taking a cycle by train could also be useful for commuters, particularly if travelling to or from an area with poor public transport. However, such a practice is no longer possible for many commuters due to restrictions introduced recently as a result of limited brake van capacity on many trains.

Charges and restrictions
On most British Rail trains cycles are now carried without charge but there are exceptions:

Western Region High Speed intercity trains to and from Paddington: child fare payable Monday to Friday.

London Midland Region services into Euston, St Pancras, Broad Street and Marylebone, Western Region services into Paddington and Eastern Region services into King's Cross: flat fare is charged on Mondays to Fridays on trains arriving at the termini between 0745 and 0945 and departing between 1630 and 1830. This only applies to journeys wholly within the London suburban area.

Continental boat trains to ports other than Harwich: various charges payable.

Cycles are not carried on the following British Rail services:

Southern Region services arriving at London termini 0745 to 0945 and departing 1630 to 1830 Monday to Friday: this applies only to journeys wholly within the London suburban area except for 'sliding door' trains, on which no cycles are then carried.

Eastern Region 'sliding door' trains to and from Finsbury Park,

Liverpool Street and Fenchurch Street: during the above times.

Finsbury Park to Moorgate and Waterloo and City line services: at any time.

Eastern Region High Speed intercity trains to and from King's Cross: daily except on Saturday afternoons and Sundays.

Isle of Wight trains: at any time.

Merseyrail suburban electric trains: during Monday to Friday peak hours and all day Saturday.

The complex regulations governing the carriage of cycles by train change from time to time and therefore it is best to check the current position before travelling. Also at weekends it is as well to check that there will not be engineering works en route as there is usually no provision for carrying cycles by substitute bus services.

London Transport
Cycles may be taken on the Metropolitan, District and Circle lines of London Transport but not on the other 'tube' lines. This is permitted Monday to Friday only between 1000 and 1600 and after 1900, but at weekends and on public holidays cycles may be taken at any time. The relevant child fare for the journey is payable for the cycle.

Joining the train
Arrive early at the station and attach a label to your machine giving your name and destination station. This is a condition of carriage and your cycle may be refused without it.

Usually cycles are carried in the brake van of a train so enquire of the ticket inspector or other station staff where along the platform this is likely to be and make your way there. Don't be tempted to ride along the platform or concourse as this can be dangerous and provokes hostility towards cyclists. Remove anything of value from the cycle and any other items you wish to keep with you well before the train is due. When the train arrives load your cycle as quickly as possible, especially if the train has no internal corridor by which to reach the passenger compartments. Position a cycle in such a way that it cannot fall over or roll when the train moves. An elastic strap can be useful for securing the machine to the side of the van or alternatively it may be used to hold on to one of the brake levers. Take care not to obstruct doors and do not chain or lock a cycle in any way as this can cause inconvenience to railway staff. When taking your seat, try to stay close to the brake van so that you can keep an eye on movements at intermediate stations and ensure that no one removes your machine.

On London Transport, Eastern and Southern Region 'sliding door' trains there are no brake vans and cycles have to be taken into the passenger compartments which makes loading particularly easy. However, it is necessary to remain with cycles inside the sliding doors to support them and keep them clear of other passengers entering and leaving.

At your destination station try to remove your cycle from the train as quickly as possible but then be patient when passing through the station barriers. It is usually a good idea to let other passengers go first.

Routes
The following routes give ideas for circular rides based on country stations which are easy to reach from London. Details are given of the London termini from which trains normally run, but most of these trains also stop at intermediate stations in the suburbs. Ask at your local station for information about times and fares.

Route 25
INGATESTONE - BURNHAM-ON-CROUCH
48 miles (76km)

Bartholomew: 1:100,000: 16
OS 1:50,000: 167, 168, 178

Train from Liverpool Street to Ingatestone. This is flat country with very easy cycling. Before setting out, note the remarks about the ferry link.

Ingatestone 15thC church with dominant tower, includes Roman bricks. Elizabethan Ingatestone Hall nearby.

Stock 16thC almshouses built by Richard Twedye. 14thC church with wooden belfry and spire and huge oak beams. Tower windmill with machinery intact.

West Hanningfield On northern edge of Hanningfield Reservoir. Church has unusual 15thC wooden belfry and, inside a 600 year old chest.

East Hanningfield On a ridge with extensive views. The oldest well in Essex is in the vicar's garden.

Althorne The church has a beautiful font with carvings of costumes worn by rich and poor about 1400. Also mediaeval scratch dial on nave buttress.

Burnham-on-Crouch Once a busy commercial port, the town is now famous as a yachting centre on the River Crouch and for its oyster fisheries.

a A passenger and cycle ferry operates between Burnham-on-Crouch and Grapnells on Wallasea Island. The service is frequent during summer, but only three or four a day in winter when there is also no Saturday or Sunday service. There is no other crossing of the River Crouch east of Battlesbridge.

Canewdon Near here was fought the battle which put the Dane, Canute, on the throne of England. The village was named after him. The large church contains Roman bricks and its tower was once used as a beacon for navigation. The organ is from the old St Paul's, and was brought here after the Great Fire of London.

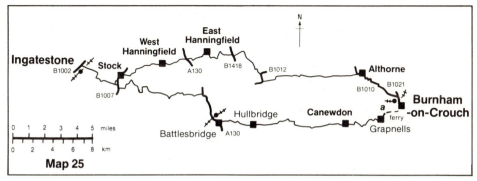

Map 25

Route 26
BISHOP'S STORTFORD - FINCHINGFIELD
45 miles (72km)

Bartholomew: 1:100,000: 16
OS 1:50,000: 167

Train from Liverpool Street to Bishop's Stortford. The countryside undulates gently with no steep hills and is ideal for cycling.

Bishop's Stortford Birthplace of Cecil Rhodes, for whom there is a memorial museum. 16th and 17thC inns with overhanging storeys. Splendid 15thC church with prominent spire.

Stansted Mountfitchet Tower windmill with machinery intact (open). Norman House wildlife park (open). London's fourth airport to SE.

Elsenham A fruit growing area. The church has a door arch made of Roman tiles.

Henham Wide greens and thatched cottages. Restored 17thC windmill at Mill Farm.

Thaxted Market town with many timbered, plastered and pargetted houses. 16thC Guildhall on stilts with lock-up beneath. The exquisite church, 183 feet long, is one of the most beautiful in Essex, rich in woodwork and glass. The 15thC carved font is unique in England. Restored tower windmill (open).

Great Bardfield Old cottages and shops, 'Gibraltar' tower windmill. Place House, 16thC, has overhanging storey. 14thC church has rare stone screen at chancel entrance. Cottage Museum.

Finchingfield Reputed to be the most beautiful village in England, set around a large green. Charming cottages, 16thC farms and splendid 12thC church. Spain's Hall is a good example of Tudor workmanship. Also post mill and timber Guildhall.

Great Dunmow Market place with 16thC town hall. Interesting church and 16thC house with timbered clock turret. Old windmill.

Great Canfield Perfect and near-original Norman church with beautiful wall painting of a Madonna. Old castle mound and moat.

Hatfield Forest Remains of ancient royal forest with magnificent hornbeams. Late Iron-Age earthwork. Picnic site, tea shop, lake for boating and fishing. NT, open.

Route 27
BISHOP'S STORTFORD - CROMER
38 miles (61km)

Bartholomew: 1:100,000:15
OS 1:50,000: 166,167

Train from Liverpool Street to Bishop's Stortford. Easy cycling country with gentle hills.

Bishop's Stortford see Route 26.

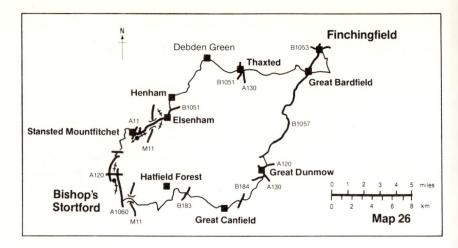

Map 26

Hadham Cross A farmhouse is the remains of the palace which was the country home of the Bishops of London for 800 years.

Benington Remains of Norman castle, with drained moat. 14thC church.

Walkern The statute against witchcraft was repealed in 1736 as a result of a case here. The church contains many brass and stone treasures.

Cromer 16thC cottages and farm. Old post mill.

Ardeley Houses and the village hall are in a horseshoe around the green.

Wood End Two farms here are 300 years old.

a Dismount to use footpath on line of old village road to the east of the A10.

Braughing see Route 9.

b The main route uses a bridleway between Braughing Friars and Albury which is easy to ride at most times. The alternative route uses a section of the busy A120.

Albury 16thC timbered house with leaning walls. 'The Labour in Vain' inn.

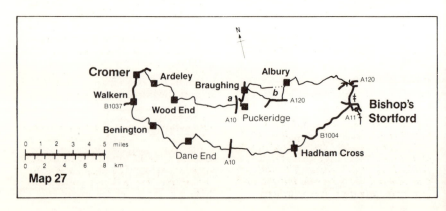

Map 27

Route 28
ST ALBAN'S - KING'S WALDEN
35 miles (56km)

Bartholomew: 1:100,000: 15
OS 1:50,000: 166

Train from St Pancras to St Albans.
Moderately hilly area with a few long
climbs out of valleys, but generally not
too difficult.

St Alban's see Route 10.

Coleman Green Small hamlet along
narrow lanes. Ford nearby at
Waterend.

Ayot St Peter Hill top village
surrounded by woods.

Ayot St Lawrence Timbered cottages
and a Georgian church with a classical
colonnade. Shaw's Corner, Bernard
Shaw's house, open Wed - Sun, and
Bank Holidays in summer: NT.
Exhibits include Shaw's CTC
membership cards. Lullingstone Silk
Farm (open) at Ayot House.

Preston John Bunyan used to preach
in Wain Wood. Churchyard has
avenues of cypresses.

King's Walden Church has beautiful
15thC screen and figures of Henry VI
and Margaret of Anjou above the
arcades.

Breachwood Green John Bunyan
used to preach in the Baptist chapel.

Wheathampstead Nomansland heath
has ancient trenches, some protected
by the NT. Mackery End is a 16thC
farmhouse, once the home of Charles
Lamb.

Childwick Green A secluded hamlet
away from the main road.

*a The route south from Childwick
Green is a bridleway. This starts as a
tarmac private road but then diverges
alongside a wood and then across open
fields. It is straightforward to follow
and generally easy to ride but the path
can be muddy after wet weather.*

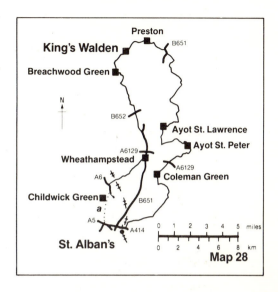

Map 28

Route 29
HARPENDEN - WOBURN
56 miles (90km)

Bartholomew: 1:100,000: 15
OS 1:50,000: 165,166

Train from St Pancras to Harpenden.
Alternatively the route can be joined at
Cheddington by train from Euston.
The route is generally quite flat but
there are some steep hills, sometimes
prolonged.

Harpenden Meaning 'valley of the
nightingales', the town has a broad
High Street and many trees. Turner's
Hall, 1665, towards Flamstead. Also
nearby is Rothamsted Agricultural
Research Station where much work on
fertilizers and crop rotation is done.
Founded by John Bennet Lawes.

Luton Airport London's third civil
airport

Lilley Birthplace of James Janeway,
17thC writer of children's books.

Streatley 14thC church with Georgian
house close by. The deep cutting on
the A6 replaced a dangerous descent in
1832.

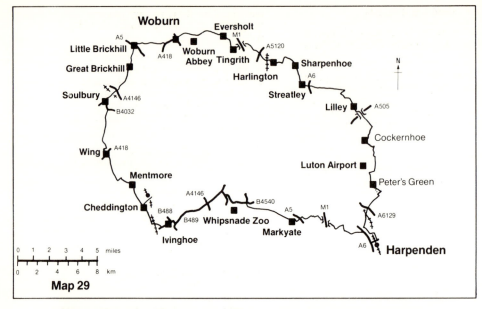

Map 29

Sharpenhoe The Clappers, the hill above the village to the south, marks the end of the Chilterns. NT. Good views. Bury Farm retains the wide moat of an earlier house.

Harlington Some half-timbered houses and old inns. The Manor House was where John Bunyan was committed for trial, subsequently to be imprisoned, after preaching nearby.

Tingrith Old houses by the church and a modern housing estate.

Eversholt Many interesting old houses, some of lath and plaster. One at Church End has a right of way through its garden. A village surrounded by 'Ends'.

Woburn Abbey Estate started by the 4th Duke of Bedford and now the location of a wildlife reserve open to the public. Woburn Abbey has many finely furnished rooms and contains an impressive collection of paintings, china, etc. Open every day of the year.

Woburn An attractive small town with much character. Market house, almshouses, old school and inns.

Little Brickhill Good views along the Ouzel valley from the church tower.

Great Brickhill On sandhills amidst pine woods. The 13thC church has beautiful mouldings.

Soulbury Village green and pond. Liscombe House, home of the local lords since the 14thC, was rebuilt in Tudor times. Interesting monuments in 14th-15C church.

Wing One of the finest 7thC Saxon churches with a well-preserved crypt. There are Roman tiles in the window and 14thC glass. Ascott House (NT: open Wed and Sat afternoons in summer) has a rich collection of French and Chippendale furniture, paintings and oriental porcelain.

Mentmore Situated on an isolated hill. The clerestoried church has a Norman font. Beautiful Mentmore House was built by Paxton and is now the centre for a religious sect. Grounds open to public.

Cheddington Saxon terraces on hills to south. A Jacobean carved oak pulpit in the church. This is a village of trees and orchards.

Ivinghoe see Route 11.

Whipsnade Large open-air zoo, a branch of London (Regent's Park) Zoo.

Markyate On the Roman Watling Street, now bypassed by main traffic. Markyate Cell is a 16thC house with stone mouldings from an earlier nunnery church on the same site.

Route 30
AMERSHAM - THE CHILTERNS
22 miles (35km)

Bartholomew: 1:100,000: 15
OS 1:50,000: 165

Train from Baker Street (Metropolitan Line) to Amersham. There are also trains from Marylebone to Amersham on weekdays. The roads along the valleys and on top of the Chilterns are reasonably flat, but hills into and out of valleys are usually steep. Nevertheless this short route provides a good introduction to cycletouring.

Amersham The Old Town, in the Misbourne valley, has many fine timber and gabled buildings. The 17thC market hall has a wooden turret and there are two watermills. Shardeloes House, one mile west, is by Robert Adam with grounds by Repton. It was the home of the Drake family to whom there are many memorials in the

church. The 18thC rectory has a timbered house with a horse-worked well.

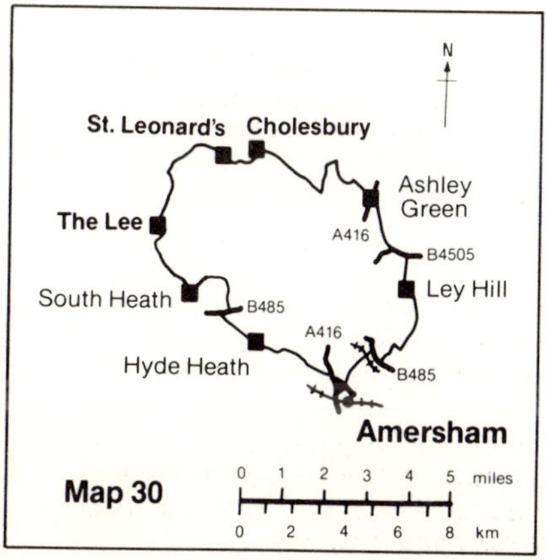

The Lee The old and new churches are within a prehistoric fort enclosure. The 13thC church has a font with staple holes for locking to prevent witches stealing the holy water. Sir Arthur Liberty, founder of the London store, is buried by the new church.

St Leonards 15thC church with pyramidal bellcot and monument to its restorer, Cornelius Wood.

Cholesbury Ancient British fortification. Also 13thC church, carefully rebuilt in 19thC.

Route 31
PRINCE'S RISBOROUGH —
WADDESDON
41 miles (65 km)

Bartholomew: 1:100,000: 15
OS 1:50,000: 165

Train from Marylebone to Prince's Risborough. This is very easy cycling country with few hills.

Prince's Risborough Many gabled and timbered houses and a quaint market house. The Mount, Saxon earthworks, NT. Manor House (NT: open Wed afternoons in summer), opposite the church, is a 17thC redbrick house with a Jacobean oak staircase and 18thC wainscoting.

Stone Thatched cottages and red-tiled barns. The Norman church has a richly carved font, previously in church at Hampstead Norris.

a The route from Stone to Waddesdon uses a private road which is coincident with a bridleway for part of the way. The road is surfaced.

Waddesdon Old houses, inn and almhouses. Waddesdon Manor (NT: open Wed-Sun afternoons, April to October) modelled on a French chateau and built by Rothschild. Battlemented church with large stone knight at

St. Leonard's Cholesbury

The Lee

South Heath

Hyde Heath

Ashley Green

A416

B4505

Ley Hill

B485

A416

B485

Amersham

Map 30

0 1 2 3 4 5 miles

0 2 4 6 8 km

chancel entrance, believed to be Sir Roger Dynham.

Quainton Spacious green, old cross and Tudor cottages. Also old windmill. Steam railway centre at Quainton Road station.

Brill On top of a 600 ft hill the site of an ancient palace. Dorton House (open), 17th-18thC, now a school. 17thC windmill. 14th-15thC church with mediaeval paintings.

Long Crendon A centre for lace-making with many 16th and 17thC cottages. Long Crendon Manor, a 15thC gabled house. Catherine's Court House (NT, open Wed, Sat and Sun afternoons April to October), 14thC, the venue for manorial courts until recently. 13thC church with magnificent tomb of Sir John Dormer and his wife.

Thame Market town with wide street and timbered houses with overhanging storeys. Bird Cage Inn, 15thC. Thame Park has been enclosed since Saxon times, the present 18thC house was built on the site of a 12thC abbey.

Chinnor Church with many famous 14thC brasses and windows. Quarrying area.

Bledlow Turf-cut cross in chalk hillside. 13thC church with three-stage tower and original doors.

Route 32
WEST DRAYTON — WRAYSBURY
23 miles (36 km)

Bartholomew: 1:100,000: 9
OS 1:50,000: 176

Train from Paddington to West Drayton & Yiewsley. The route may also be joined at Wraysbury by train from Waterloo. This is a very flat route, for easy cycling, close to London, but it does cross a number of busy roads and pass through some urban areas.

West Drayton Impressive gatehouse and walls are all that remains of Manor House. Large green with character. Elaborate octagonal font in parish church of St Martin.

Colnbrook see Route 14.

Wraysbury Surrounded by reservoirs. An old ford remains.

Iver see Route 13.

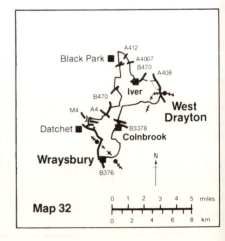

Map 31 / Map 32

Route 33
TWYFORD — EAST ILSLEY
57 miles (91 km)

Bartholomew: 1:100,000:8
OS 1:50,000: 174, 175

Train from Paddington to Twyford.
Generally a hilly route, some of the
hills being steep.

Twyford 17thC almshouses. 19thC
church, built of 13thC style, has
coloured marbles on the floor of the
baptistry.

Mapledurham A Thames-side village
situated under wooded hills. River mill
with wooden wheel and church with an
old oak nave roof and an old fire
engine from 1743. Mapledurham
House, built by Sir Michael Blount, is
one of the finest Tudor houses in
England. Open.

*a The main route uses a bridleway
along the Thames valley, passing
Hardwick House. It is usually easy to
ride.*

Pangbourne Nautical college on hill,
established 1917. Toll bridge over
Thames, cycles free. Attractive views
by river.

Hermitage Grimsbury Castle nearby is
a prehistoric earthwork. The 19thC
church, in Early English style, was
founded by Queen Adelaide.

Chieveley Church with unusual fine
oak arch across chancel. Pulpit with
Jacobean carving.

Peasemore Among woods, the church
has some interesting modern glass.

East Ilsley A village in a deep hollow
in the Berkshire Downs. The church,
part 12thC, has an unusual nine-sided
font.

West Ilsley Attractive old houses,
barns and church.

*b An alternative route back to
Streatley is along The Ridgeway: a long
distance bridleway from Streatley to
near Avebury. The surface is
predominantly chalk, which can be
very slippery when wet, and is often
well-rutted. However, with low gears it
is quite easy to cycle but much slower
than the road route.*

Compton Ancient earthworks nearby.
Small flint church, much modernized.

Aldworth Church dominated by the
large tombs of the de la Beche family,
once local landowners.

Streatley Attractive bridge across the
Thames. There are extensive views of
the Chilterns, Thames valley and
Goring Gap from Lardon Chase and
Lough Down above the town (NT).

Goring Where the Icknield Way, the
oldest road in England, crosses the

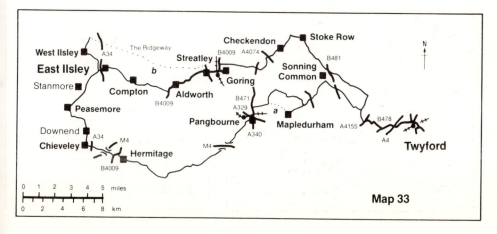

Map 33

Thames. The Norman church has a late 13thC bell.

Checkendon: High Chiltern village with timbered cottages around a green.

Stoke Row The attractive well, in a house with a dome, was given to the village by the Maharajah of Benares in 1864.

Sonning Common Nearby are Crowsley Deer Park with a Jacobean house and Rotherfield Peppard where the church has beautiful woodwork.

Route 34
WOKINGHAM — STRATFIELD SAYE
43 miles (69 km)

Bartholomew: 1:100,000: 8
OS 1:50,000: 175

Train from Waterloo to Wokingham. For the most part a flat route, with no hills of great severity. Easy cycling.

Wokingham Once the site of a bell foundry and later a silk industry. There are a few old cottages and overhanging houses and a 19thC town hall with portraits of monarchs and dukes. A curfew bell is tolled on winter nights.

Mattingley 15thC timber-framed church with rare 17thC altar frontal.

Bramley Attractive church of brick, stucco and flint. Striking 16thC pews. 13thC wall painting of the murder of Thomas à Becket.

The Vyne Lovely Tudor house with two long galleries. Earliest classical portico on any English country house. Restored. (NT,) open Tu, Wed, Thu, Sat and Sun afternoons April to October.

Sherborne St John Church has nave and chancel built in one and copper spire on the spiky west tower.

Monk Sherborne Early Norman church. Another church at Pamber End is the remains of Monk Sherborne Priory, founded in the 12thC.

Little London Two miles north is the site of Roman Calleva Atrebatum. Parts of the outer wall remain.

Stratford Saye Originally owned by the Pitt family, the estate was given to the first Duke of Wellington by the nation in 1817 in thanks for the victory of Waterloo. The house dates from 1630 but is not open.

a The alternative route keeps to attractive narrow lanes but requires carrying cycles over a low footbridge to bypass a deep ford.

Farley Hill Farley Hill House built by the founders of *The Times*. The church has a spire out of its side.

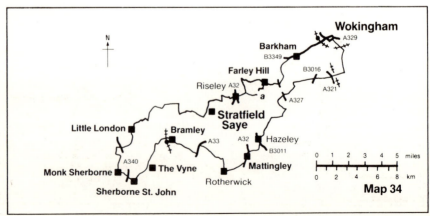

Map 34

Barkham The Ball family, ancestors of George Washington, are buried in the churchyard.

Route 35
FARNCOMBE - ODIHAM
55 miles (88km)

Bartholomew: 1:100,000: 9
OS: 1:50,000: 186

Train from Waterloo to Farncombe. A fairly long and hilly ride but in beautiful countryside.

Farncombe Twin town with Godalming. See Route 16.

Puttenham Attractive church with Norman arches and modern oak carving. Shoelands, one mile west, is an interesting Tudor house.

Seale Village under the Hog's Back. The church has an impressive porch. East End Farm includes a 16thC timber house with unusual chimneys.

Farnham Many attractive old houses and large church with many memorials. Town Museum at Wilmer House. William Corbett born at the 'Jolly Farmer' and buried in the churchyard. Castle (DoE, open) includes rare original Norman woodwork and was formerly the home of the bishops of Winchester for over 800 years.

Crondall Spectacular Norman church. Tall brick tower copied from Battersea church and situated unusually on the north side of the chancel. Village with narrow streets.

Odiham An attractive and mainly Georgian town whose wide main street has many buildings of high architectural standard. Almshouses, old stocks, whipping post. Remains of the 13thC keep of Odiham Castle: the only octagonal keep in England. King John was in refuge here when forced to accept the *Magna Carta*. Basingstoke Canal tunnel to the west.

Binsted On a belt of Upper Greensand in a charming unspoilt area. The village church is of high standard with distinguished arcades.

Thursley Picturesque cottages. Church with 15thC wooden belfry and many Saxon treasures including an oven and large font. Sad epitaph on tombstone to unknown sailor in churchyard.

Hambledon A village amidst narrow lanes. The churchyard has large yew trees. Good views from Hydon's Ball hill (NT) nearby.

Hascombe Mediaeval screen in church made from olive trees. Fine views from Hascombe Hill. Winkworth Arboretum (NT, open daily) is a wooded garden around two lakes with many rare trees and shrubs.

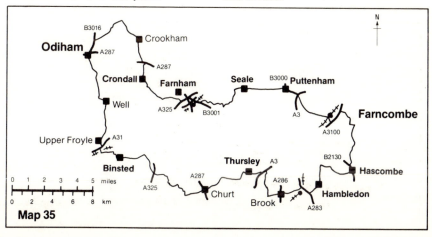

Map 35

Route 36
OXTED — EAST GRINSTEAD
44 miles (70 km)

Bartholomew: 1:100,000: 9
OS 1:50,000: 187, 188

Train from Victoria to Oxted. The northern part of this route is fairly flat but it becomes hillier towards and across the Sussex border.

Oxted Steep old street with 17thC and 18thC cottages and old timbered inn at the top. Ancient church with great low tower.

Lingfield St Peter's Cross, the village lock-up and restored boundary mark, is now a simple museum. A house with stone roof west of the church is on the site of a 15thC college and there are other pretty buildings nearby. Church with very rich collection of monuments, particularly of the lords of Starborough Castle. War memorial at Plaistow Street has an everburning light. Racecourse to south of town.

East Grinstead Handsome town at the eastern end of the Forest Ridge.

Wide High Street with ancient timber and plaster houses. Sackville College, 17thC almshouses, is one of the finest Jacobean buildings in England. Queen Victoria Hospital is famous for plastic surgery.

Turner's Hill A crossroads village high up on the Forest Ridge.

West Hoathly A high village with good views north and south. The part 11thC church with a shingled spire is visible for miles. The 15thC Priest's House has a perfect Horsham slab roof on timber-frame walls and is now a folk museum arranged as an 18thC dwelling house. 'Big-on-Little', a rock formation with a large rock precariously balanced on one much smaller, is nearby.

Forest Row The capital of Ashdown Forest with a mixture of ancient and modern. The forest itself, to the south, is in fact more moorland than woodland now and is the home of many wild flowers, some of which are rare.

a From Forest Row to Ball's Green near Withyham it is possible to follow the track of the old railway line which is now a walking, horse riding and cycling route. The surface is mostly ash and quite easy to ride but in some places after wet weather it can be muddy. The alternative route by road is much hillier.

Hartfield A pleasant village, the church lychgate is attached to the side of a 16thC cottage.

Withyham An Arcadian village complete with lake. The church has a 17thC Sackville chapel and monument.

Markbeech A high hamlet with good views north to the Greensand Hills and south across the Weald.

Hever Tudor inn with interesting Henry VIII sign. Church with 14thC tower, barrel roof, shingle spire, Jacobean pulpit and good brasses. Hever Castle, a moated Tudor manor, was often visited by Henry VIII. Restored and filled with Renaissance paintings and other treasures. Open.

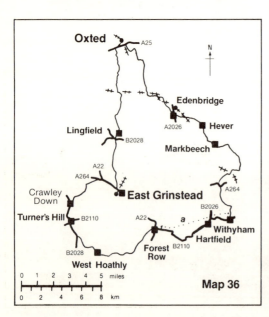

Map 36

Edenbridge An old town with character and a number of old houses. Light industries include tanneries and flour mills.

**Route 37
EYNSFORD —
NORTH DOWNS WAY
37 miles (60 km)**

Bartholomew: 1:100,000: 10
OS 1:50,000: 177, 188

Train from Holborn Viaduct or Blackfriars to Eynsford on Mondays to Fridays, from Victoria to Eynsford at weekends. This is a route with a difference, being an introduction to 'rough stuff' cycling. Use is made of a number of bridleways, RUPPs and unrestricted footpaths and the southern section of the route is coincident with the North Downs Way and Pilgrim's Way. Most of the tracks are quite easy to ride on a cycle equipped with reasonably low gears but great care is necessary on steep sections and some mud is inevitable particularly after wet weather. Care should be exercised too along the narrow roads as there are a number of steep hills here. Use of the Ordnance Survey 1:50,000 maps is recommended to follow the tracks, but

a compass is not essential. Note that the accompanying line map is drawn to a larger scale than the others in this section of the book This is an enjoyable route, away from traffic, for the more experienced cyclist.

Eynsford see Route 20.

Farningham see Route 22.

West Kingsdown Dominated by the busy A20 road, this town has a preserved and restored windmill, an old-fashioned village post office and a Norman tower. Brand's Hatch motor racing circuit is to the north.

Stansted The Old Malt House, on the road to Ash, displays 15thC building with mud and straw. Unusual war memorial.

Ridley Secluded village with thatched well, manor house and large Norman church.

a Track from near South Street to Harvel.

b Footpath track around Holly Hill.

c RUPP. The route diverges from the North Downs Way towards Great Buckland.

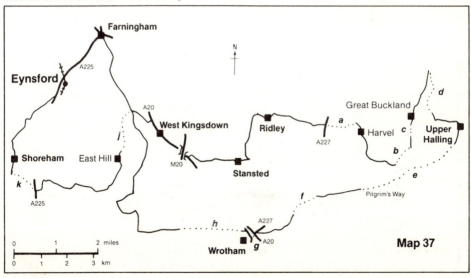

Map 37

d RUPP by Hatch Hill and to west of Horseholders Wood.

Upper Halling Cottages incorporate the walls of an old chapel. 'Halling Man' was discovered near here in 1912. Originally thought to be 25,000 years old, but subsequently proved to be only 4,000 years old. Now in the British Museum.

e Route follows the Pilgrim's Way, part RUPP, part bridleway.

f RUPP around hillside after Pilgrim House.

g Dismount to use short footpath along line of old A227 from A20 roundabout to Wrotham village .

Wrotham An old village built around a square. The church east window is from St Alban's Wood Street in London and there are fine brasses. An old processional way, now a footpath, passes through Wrotham Tower. From Wrotham Hill to the north there is a fine view of the Weald.

h RUPP along Pilgrim's Way.

j Bridleway through High Castle Wood.

k RUPP north of Filston Hill.

Shoreham see Route 22.

10. CYCLE PARKING

Take care when leaving your cycle, as every year over 18,000 machines are stolen in London; and even in the country areas around the capital cycle theft rates are high.

Although virtually nothing will stop a determined thief, most cycle thefts are carried out by 'opportunists', who can be deterred by the simple expedient of locking the cycle to a fixed object. Even the professionals will usually take an adjacent unlocked machine rather than trouble with locks or bolt cutters. Therefore for any cyclist a good lock is essential and it should be used every time the cycle is left, no matter for how short a time. Preferably buy a stout hardened steel chain together with a separate lock of a type having a large number of key permutations. Although more expensive than a combined lock and chain, there will be much less chance of anyone else having a key to fit it.

Leave your cycle only in busy, well-observed places; not at the side or rear of shops or other buildings. Unsupervised car parks are generally unsuitable as many cycles are stolen by loading into a car or van, lock and all. Remove all accessories and loop the lock chain through at least the front wheel and the frame and then around a lamppost, railing, tree or other fixed object. Take care, however, that you do not leave your machine in any place where it could cause inconvenience to pedestrians, particularly those who are blind. If cycle parking stands are provided be wary of types which grip the cycle by one or both wheels as these can cause damage if the cycle is knocked or heavily laden.

If you need to leave your cycle for a long period, try to put it behind a locked door or near someone such as a commissionaire or car park attendant who might be asked to keep an eye on it. In central London there is an official supervised cycle park at Poland Street garage, off Oxford Street. Here machines can be left in safety for a small fee and there are also cycle lockers available to give added protection to luggage and accessories. The cycle park is open daily from 0600 to midnight, 0100 Sundays.

In the City of London cycles may be left free of charge in all Corporation car parks but here supervision is not guaranteed, although one can always ask.

Facilities for leaving cycles are also available at the Left Luggage offices of most British Rail terminal stations in central London and at some of the larger stations in the suburbs. Some of these facilities are, however, fully utilized by commuters overnight and at weekends but there will usually be room during the day. Again a charge is levied although in return British Rail do accept some responsibility for cycles stored.

A number of other stations have cycle parking racks which are unsupervised and where parking is free but these suffer badly from vandalism and theft, especially when sited away from the main station buildings.

Just in case you are unlucky enough to have your cycle stolen, it is very important to keep a good description of it to give to the police. Note the make, model, colour, frame number -often stamped either under the bottom bracket or on the rear wheel dropout -and any other distinguishing features. If your cycle is not numbered, most dealers will do this for you.

It is also advisable to take out adequate insurance cover so that at least you do not suffer financially as a result of any loss. Most insurance companies will quote for cycle theft insurance as well as for other types such as personal accident and third party (liability to others) which it is advisable to have. Cycling organizations such as the CTC also operate competitive insurances for their members.

11. ORGANIZED CYCLING

Touring

Riding in the company of others adds a new dimension to cycling and can be very enjoyable. As well as making new friends with similar interests, there is much to be learnt from the experiences of others and riding in a group can also be easier, particularly in bad weather.

There are a number of cycling clubs around London which organize local cycletouring and social events including Sections of the Cyclists' Touring Club. Rides into the countryside take place every Sunday and some weekdays, using the quieter roads and tracks away from traffic and often visiting places of interest. Meeting places, usually the start of cycle runs by CTC sections include:

Central London (frequently using trains to skip the suburbs), Ardleigh Green, Brentwood, Bromley, Chingford, Chislehurst, Croydon, Ealing, Edgware, Enfield, Heston, Kidbrooke, Mitcham, North Cheam, Orpington, Putney Heath, Ruislip, Sidcup, Uxbridge, West Drayton and West Wickham.

There are also tours to places further afield at holiday times, competitions and clubroom evenings with slide shows, talks, maintenance sessions, etc. Details of local CTC activities can be obtained through CTC Headquarters (see Appendix C) and information on other cycling clubs can usually be found in public libraries.

When riding with others it is advisable to fit a rear mudflap to prevent road spray hitting riders behind.

Urban cycling

The local District Associations of the CTC undertake extensive work towards improving conditions for all cyclists in London by negotiating with the boroughs and Greater London Council to complement the national Club's work with Government departments. The CTC is the official consultative body for cycling recognized by the Government and GLC and makes representation on new traffic schemes and area plans to ensure that the cyclist's view is not overlooked. The Club has been involved with most of the new schemes now being introduced to help cyclists in the capital and has been responsible for initiating many. Assistance towards this important work is always welcomed and enquiries can be directed through CTC Headquarters.

Similar work is also carried out by a number of independent cycling clubs in London and there are also local pressure groups promoting cycling in some areas.

Cycle sport

Track and road racing and time trialing are popular sports in London and there are opportunities to take part in these activities either as participants or spectators.

Regular cycle racing meetings are held during the season at the following venues:

Track Racing: Herne Hill Cycle Track, Burbage Road SE24. Monday evenings and some weekends. Paddington Recreation Ground, Grantully Road W9. Tuesday evenings and some weekends.

Road Racing: Crystal Palace Park, SE19. Tuesday evenings. Eastway Cycle Track, Temple Mills Lane, E15. Thursday evenings and weekends. There are also occasional road racing events at Battersea Park and Finsbury Park.

Many cycling clubs in London organize their own racing events and time trials, as well as competing in League events. It is necessary to join one of these clubs in order to participate in cycle sport. Details can be obtained from the coordinating bodies: the British Cycling Federation and the Road Time Trials Council (see Appendix C).

APPENDIX A STARTING OUT

Cycling is an uncomplicated activity, which can give freedom, peace, exhilarating exercise and adventure as well as being a most sane and practical form of transport. However, as with most things, knowledge of a few basic principles about equipment and technique can make cycling so much easier and more pleasant. This starts when buying a machine.

Choosing a bicycle

It is always best to buy a cycle, whether new or secondhand, from an accredited specialist cycle dealer. Here you will receive expert advice and guidance as well as being assured of good after-sales service and the availability of spares. Discount houses and chain stores may seem cheaper at first, but their staff may know little about cycling and it is sometimes difficult to get replacement parts for cheap cycles.

Small-wheeled cycles may be fine for short shopping trips and the folding types can be useful for the commuter travelling part of the way by car or train. However, these machines are too low and cumbersome for enjoyable cycling over longer distances and standard size bicycles are generally to be preferred. Before going to a shop, measure your inside leg (from crotch to heel on the floor) and subtract ten inches. Ask for a bike with this frame size. There are not many ladies' cycles larger than 21-inch frame, so taller women may have to shop around if they do not want to buy a man's machine. In practice many women actually prefer a man's model as the frame is inherently stronger and more responsive.

Even frames of similar height vary in length and other details so try several. A wrong decision at this stage could force you to ride with stomach cramped, back bent or legs unable to provide enough power. If necessary ask for a longer or shorter handlebar extension to compensate for variations in frame length. Most dealers will be pleased to attend to these details.

Enthusiasts spend hundreds of pounds on their machines, selecting individual components with an untiring dedication to detail. Such perfectionism does indeed have its rewards in easier cycling, particularly over long distances and in hilly country, but it would be very wrong to think that it is necessary to go to these lengths to enjoy cycling. In fact what makes an 'ideal' cycle is very much a matter of personal preference, so even a newcomer, with money to spare, would be well advised to ascertain his preferences on something more modest. Nonetheless there are certain features which it is wise for every cyclist to pay careful attention to.

Probably the most important asset a cycle can have is a good set of gears for it is gearing which makes the most difference to how easy a cycle is to ride. This is no less true in London, even though the area is generally flat, for gears are as important in traffic as for climbing hills. Ask your dealer to change these if necessary so that there is a range at least from about 40 inches to 85 inches: lower than 40 inches if you intend to do a lot of hill climbing. (Cycle gears are specified in inches and relate to the diameter of a fixed wheel which would cover the same ground in one revolution of the pedals. Your dealer will understand the figures quoted and will be able to explain further). Five or ten speed derailleur gears are the most popular with cyclists and can be obtained most easily with wide ratios, but three and four speed hub gears also have their advocates, being generally cleaner and easier to maintain. They also have the advantage of being able to be changed when the cycle is stationary. Single-speed cycles are really only suitable for the super-fit.

Although it adds a little more to a cycle's cost, alloy rimmed wheels are also well worth acquiring. As well as being lighter than steel ones and rust-free, alloy wheels are much better for braking and this can be very important. Buy standard alloy rims, not the so-called narrow section ones which are best left to the experts. Ensure, too, that the wheels are equipped with tyres having a good tread for these will stand up to road wear much better than smooth racing tyres. If buying secondhand, pay particular attention to the condition of tyres and brakes.

Many people are put off cycles with dropped handlebars because of their racing image. This is unfortunate: only the rider makes a cycle race, not its handlebars! In fact dropped bars are the most comfortable as they allow for a variety of riding positions. As they are less wide than straight bars they can also be safer in traffic, provided that they are not too low and that fingers can reach the brake levers comfortably, although these can be adjusted in position to some extent.

Another component dismissed by many is toe clips. Contrary to first reactions, these can actually make cycling safer and there is no problem removing a foot in a hurry so long as the straps are not kept too tight. Toe clips aid pedalling by preventing shoes from slipping forward and in traffic one clip is invaluable for repositioning the pedals quickly after a hurried stop. However, new cyclists would probably be better to become confident in the control of their cycle before adding toe clips and then they should perhaps use only one for a little while.

Some cycles, particularly ladies' models, come with saddles which are too wide for optimum comfort. They can chafe and bounce and much pedalling effort is then lost in the springs. Seek something firmer before leaving the shop. Generally leather saddles are preferred by experienced cyclists, but some of the modern nylon ones are very good and have the advantages of being cheaper and rain resistant. All saddles take some time to wear in, so be prepared for a little discomfort at first.

Carrying luggage

Always fix luggage to the bike, not to yourself. In particular never carry anything on your back as this can affect balance and be dangerous should it shift. A wide variety of saddlebags, baskets and panniers are available for utility or touring purposes and cycle trailers are becoming popular once more for larger loads. A strong rear carrier is important for touring to keep bulky bags clear of the mudguard and is also useful for strapping awkward packages about town. Take care to purchase a good quality rigid model.

To carry a child, a seat can be fitted at the back. The child's feet must always be safely in rests and a young child needs harnessing much as in a pushchair. Endeavour to place your own weight forward, perhaps with a longer handlebar extension or lower handlebars. This helps to counteract the child's weight.

Clothing

Generally wear loose, comfortable clothing, for cycling helps to keep you warm even in the middle of winter. Several firms specialize in cyclists' jackets which, like cycle shoes, are specially tailored to be functional as well as smart. However, many everyday garments can also be suitable, particularly for short journeys. Hooded jackets can be hazardous unless fitted tightly to the head as a cyclist must be able to make frequent glances behind for safety. A balaclava is probably more suitable for winter use.

When the weather is warm enough, shorts are undoubtedly the most comfortable lower garment and are now seen as frequently in London as in the country. Even when it rains legs can be dried much more quickly than trousers. At other times many cyclists find track suits comfortable and for women about town, worn over a dress they look tidy on the road and can be slipped off at the destination. Try to obtain styles cut for cycling, with a narrower leg, rather than the wider ones for athletes. Jeans are not suitable for riding far as they hold water in the rain and do not keep legs warm. Flare-bottomed trousers can also be difficult to keep clear of the chain.

When it does rain, many cyclists prefer a cape as this can keep all but the head and lower legs dry, together with much of the cycle including relatively sensitive components such as gear levers and saddle. However, on a windy day lighter-weight capes can be hazardous so new riders may prefer a waterproof jacket and leggings. These are only really suitable for shorter journeys as condensation is more of a problem and leggings reduce considerably pedalling efficiency.

Ready for the road

Most local authorities run cycling training schemes for children and a few also do so for adults. If you are new to cycling you may be able to take advantage of these. Alternatively you might ask an experienced cyclist for some practical guidance. However, safe, competent and enjoyable cycling is not difficult but largely a matter of practice.

Having obtained a cycle, adjust the saddle so that your toes can reach the road on both sides and the handlebars for a straight back at about 45° to the road. As you come to relax on the bike you may find it more comfortable to raise the saddle further; theoretically your leg should be straight with the *heel* on the pedal. Remember that saddles can be moved forwards and backwards too. Check that the brakes are correctly adjusted so that the blocks come into contact with the wheels with only a small movement of the brake levers. Also check tyre pressures, as soft tyres waste effort, and are more liable to puncture and wear out quickly. Tyres should be pumped hard and a tyre pressure gauge is a useful accessory as most people underinflate. 65 to 70 lb per sq inch is about right for high pressure tyres.

When pedalling, use the ball of the foot on each pedal and *ankle* the pedals round. Toe clips make this easier by ensuring the correct foot position. Feel the pull in your shoulders and remain seated. Standing on the pedals interrupts momentum and makes you a hazard to other road users. If you need to stand then either your saddle is too low or your gear too high, or both. With sufficiently low gears cyclists can climb any hill seated.

Whether you are riding across town or into the country, time spent planning and noting a quiet route, avoiding main roads, is worth every moment and the advice in the section of this book on 'Cycling in Traffic' should be followed.

As in most activities, cyclists improve in performance with practice. A mile or two every day will greatly increase the enjoyment of a longer ride. This is why the cyclist who rides to work regularly should find little difficulty in extending his or her riding for pleasure. When undertaking shorter excursions there is no need to conform to any particular routine. Stops at places of interest will usually be sufficiently frequent and the distances between not too arduous. If you need to cover a longer distance set yourself a minimum number of miles to be covered each hour, allowing for becoming more tired towards the end of the ride, and try not to do less. Planning a route well beforehand will help to minimize the number of times you need to consult a map. However, do not aim beyond your capabilities. Be patient and build up distances slowly and steadily, learning to use your ankles and low gears.

A cyclist may need no petrol, but he or she does need fuel in the form of food, particularly protein. If you are going out for the day you will probably need to carry, or buy, a larger lunch than usual. Even on short rides you should carry some spare rations in the form of chocolate, dates, etc. just in case the pangs of hunger strike when you are not near a shop. Also carry sufficient money for emergencies: you may need to catch a train home.

It is also important that you should always carry a repair outfit and tools. This is essential for any journey more than a few minutes walk away. Take a puncture repair kit, at least two tyre levers, a spare inner tube (in case a puncture is irrepairable), a multi-spanner suitable for every nut on your cycle, spare gear and brake cables, brake blocks, pliers and a screwdriver. Also don't forget a pump. If you are going further afield other items such as a freewheel remover and crank remover/installer (if you have cotterless cranks) or cotter pins (if you haven't) are useful. Familiarize yourself with the routine adjustments necessary to keep any cycle in good condition. To repair a puncture remember to remove whatever caused it, clean thoroughly the area around the hole with sandpaper and use two thin layers of rubber solution, allowing each in turn to dry, before applying the patch.

Cycling alone is an ideal way to feel and experience London or the countryside and you will usually find that people are always willing to stop and talk to a cyclist. But much can be learned by riding with others, especially a club group of like-minded people who will be on hand if you have a puncture or suffer mechanical trouble. Even a buckled wheel can be straightened in a drain cover: a remedy you might not have thought of alone!

Joining a national cycling organization such as the CTC is beneficial, as much for the town rider as the tourist, for benefits include free third party insurance and legal aid as well as lending support to the extensive negotiations which take place between the Club and local and national government for improving conditions for all cyclists.

APPENDIX B GOOD CYCLING

The bicycle is an inoffensive and unobtrusive machine which has much less effect on people and the surroundings than other vehicles. Nonetheless cyclists still have responsibilities to others, both drivers and pedestrians, and the good cyclist will treat them with the same consideration as he would like to receive himself.

Pedestrians are particularly vulnerable, even to a cycle, and cyclists are obliged to give way to pedestrians crossing the road, including when making turns. It is illegal and dangerous for cyclists to ride on the pavements and footways which border roads and those who do so cause much antagonism to pedestrians, especially the elderly, and they are the reason why some special measures to help cyclists have been refused. Likewise cyclists are not permitted to ride in parks except where this is expressly allowed (see 'Cycling in London Parks' section of this book). Cyclists may cycle, without any specific right to do so, on some footpaths which are not alongside roads provided that they do not cause a nuisance and that there is no displayed 'No Cycling' sign backed by a local authority bye-law or traffic order. Most footpaths in the London urban area are restricted. Under the Countryside Act 1968 cyclists have a right to use most bridleways and RUPPs (roads used as public paths) although in doing so they must give precedence to horse riders and walkers.

The Highway Code applies to cyclists as well as to motorists and its guidelines are worth following. There are also legal requirements which cyclists must adhere to.

Cyclists must obey all traffic signals and signs, including one-way directions, and stop when required to do so by a police officer or traffic warden in uniform. It is an offence to ride recklessly, dangerously, without due care and attention or without reasonable consideration for other persons using the road. A cyclist may be charged, in appropriate circumstances, with riding under the influence of drink or drugs although there is no obligation to submit to a breathalyser test as the relevant legislation applies only to motor vehicles. It is forbidden to hold on to a motor vehicle or trailer in motion.

Most cycles are required to have two efficient independent brakes and at night, working front and rear lights — the latter bearing the British Standard marking BS3648 — and a red rear reflector. The carrying of a passenger is prohibited unless the cycle is specially built or adapted for that purpose.

In addition to the privileges gained by a cycle being classified a vehicle, cyclists are being accorded other rights. Cyclists may use with-flow bus lanes but not contra-flow bus lanes except the one in New Oxford Street. A number of contra-flow cycles-only lanes are also being introduced. 'No Motor Vehicle' signs (motorcycle and car in red circle) controlling restricted access streets such as Oxford Street and many residential areas may be disregarded by cyclists who may also use roads such as the western side of Trafalgar Square which have blue

'Buses, Cycles and Taxis Only' signs. Many road closures in London now incorporate special gaps for cyclists although, unfortunately, not all of these are signed. Although general waiting restrictions apply to cycles as well as motor vehicles, bicycles (but not tricycles) may stop on roads with double white lines in the centre.

Other important signs relating specially to cycles are:

No Cycling: black cycle in red circle.

Route for pedal cycles only: white cycle on circular blue background.

Advisory route for cycles which may also be used by other vehicles: white cycle on rectangular blue background.

Shared cycle/pedestrian path, unsegregated: white cycle and pedestrian symbols on circular blue background.

Shared cycle/pedestrian path, segregated: as above but with line between symbols. Cyclists must keep to their appropriate part of the path.

Some other new signs also incorporate the cycle symbol and are usually self-explanatory.

APPENDIX C ORGANIZATIONS & ADDRESSES

Cycling

Cyclists' Touring Club, 69 Meadrow, Godalming, Surrey, GU7 3HS. Godalming (048 68)7217. This is the largest national cycling organization which has taken the lead for over 100 years in looking after the interests of all who ride bicycles, whether for utility or pleasure. The CTC acts at all levels from local council to Parliament to ensure that the needs and rights of cyclists are taken fully into account in both town and country.

The CTC aims to promote cycling as an enjoyable and healthy recreation for persons of all ages, urges the encouragement of the bicycle for town

transport and maintains constant vigilance in safeguarding cyclists' interests, their status on roads and bridleways, facilities for touring and access to the beauty of the countryside.

Membership benefits include free third party insurance and legal aid, *Cycletouring* magazine and local activities.

British Cycling Federation, 70 Brompton Road, London, SW3. The official body regulating cycle racing in Britain.

Road Time Trials Council: Secretary: D E Roberts, Dallacre, Mill Road, Yarwell, Peterborough. The regulating body for time trial events in Britain.

Rough Stuff Fellowship: Secretary:
F E Goatcher, 65 Stoneleigh Avenue,
Worcester Park, Surrey, KT4 8XY. An
organization for cyclists who love the
byways and tracks.

Tandem Club: Secretary: D Hasted,
54 Penhurst Road, Bedhampton,
Havant, Hants: For all tandemists,
benefits include a spares service.

Audax UK: Secretary: A J Nicholas,
188 Runcorn Road, Moore,
Warrington, Lancs: An organizing
body for long-distance reliability rides.

Tourist information

London Tourist Board:
26 Grosvenor Gardens, SW1.
01-730 0791.
Victoria Station. Personal callers only.
4th Floor, Harrod's, Brompton Road,
SW1. Personal callers only.
Ground floor, Selfridge's, Oxford
Street, W1. Personal callers only.
Heathrow Airport, Terminal 2.
Personal callers only.

City of London Information Office:
St Paul's churchyard, EC4.
01-606 3030.

**Teletourist (recorded information
on events in London):**
in English 01-246 8041
in French 01-246 8043
in German 01-246 8045

in Italian 01-246 8049
in Spanish 01-246 8047

British Tourist Authority:
64 St James's Street, SW1.
01-499 9325.

Information can also be obtained by
contacting the Town Halls of London
boroughs.

Youth hostels

Youth Hostels Association (England
& Wales), Trevelyan House, 8 St
Stephen's Hill, St Albans, Herts.
St Albans 55215. (for London hostels
see Appendix F)

Embassies and High Commissions

Australia: Australia House, Strand,
WC2. 01-438 8000
Canada: Canada House, Trafalgar
Square, SW1. 01-629 9492
France: 58 Knightsbridge, SW1.
01-235 8080
Germany (West): 22 Belgrave Square,
SW1. 01-235 5033
New Zealand: New Zealand House,
Haymarket, SW1. 01-930 8422
Netherlands: 38 Hyde Park Gate,
SW7. 01-584 5040
United States: 24 Grosvenor Square,
W1. 01-499 9000
The addresses of other embassies can
be obtained from the telephone
directory.

APPENDIX D CYCLE HIRE

Hiring a cycle for a day or weekend
can be a good way of sampling the
delights of cycling, although do
remember that cycling becomes easier
and more enjoyable with regular
practice. Hiring a cycle may also be
advantageous to a commuter if his own
machine has to be off the road for
maintenance.

The following shops in London hire
cycles. Some offer a wide range of
bicycles and tandems whilst others
have only a few small-wheeled
machines available. It is best to check
your requirements by telephone first
and during the summer advance
booking may sometimes be necessary.

For hours of opening, see Appendix E.
N10 Hill Cycles, Fortis Green Road 01-883 4644
NW4 Hendon Cycles, 23 Bell Lane 01-203 2256
NW6 Beta Bikes, 275 West End Lane 01-794 4133
NW9 Clarke, 509 Kingsbury Road 01-204 4165
SW1 Bicycle Revival, 17 Elizabeth Street 01-730 6716

SW4 Peter's Cycles, 118 Ferndale Road 01-274 5892
SW7 Rent-a-Bike, 3 Kendrick Mews 01-581 2044
SW11 Saville, 97 Battersea Rise 01-288 4279
SW19 Smith Bros, 14 Church Road, Wimbledon Village 01-946 2270
W3 Rent-a-Bike, Student Centre, Kensington Church Street 01-937 6089
Barking Vickers, 39 London Road 01-594 2703
Enfield Broadway Bikes, 65 Windmill Hill 01-367 6690
Northolt Viscount, 492 Church Road 01-845 6144
Orpington Ken Bird, 35 High Street, Green Street Green (66) 53746
West Wickham Toplis Engineering, 17 Ravenswood Crescent 01-777 1084
Whyteleafe Enquire Within, 244 Godstone Road (Upr Warlingham 820) 4059

APPENDIX E: CYCLE SHOPS' DIRECTORY

The following list, which is not exhaustive, details cycle shops in and close to London which operate a comprehensive sales, spares and repairs service. However, the range of cycles and spares stocked varies considerably from shop to shop, and some establishments do not handle lightweight components. Also many shops are often very busy with pre-booked local repairs and cannot necessarily provide on-the-spot service. It is best, therefore, to telephone first to see whether a particular shop can meet your requirements.

Shops are listed in order of postal districts and names are sometimes abbreviated. Unless otherwise stated opening hours apply Mondays to Saturdays although hours can vary, especially during school holidays. Lunch hour closing, where applicable, has not been indicated.
ADC: All day closing
ECD: Early closing day

Greater London

E2 Daycock, 201 Roman Road 01-980 4966		1000-1800, ADC Th
E4 Bakers, 92 Old Church Road 01-529 0650		0900-1730, ECD Th
Heales, 477 Hale End Road 01-527 1592		1000-1400; 1530-1800. ECD Th
James, 99 Station Road 01-524 0063	0900-1800 (1730 Sat),	1000-1300 Sun
Reliable, 32 Station Road 01-529 2780		0830-1800, ECD Th
E6 Grimstead, 427 Barking Road 01-472 0918		0930-1800
E8 McCall, 185 Mare Street 01-985 2653		1030-1730, ECD Th
Waller, 325 Kingsland Road 01-254 3792		1200-1830, ADC Th
E10 Ditchfield, 790 High Road 01-539 2821		0900-1730, ECD Th
E12 Kimberley, 696 Romford Road 01-478 1176		0900-1730, ECD Th
E13 Bates, 589 Barking Road 01-472 3483		0900-1800
E14 Roberts, 241 East India Dock Road 01-987 2922		0900-1815, ECD Th
E15 Martins Mart, 159 Leytonstone Road 01-534 1166		0900-1730
Reads, 66 Portway 01-534 5055	0900-1800 (1730 Wed, Sat),	0900-1300 Sun
E17 Bellchamber, 80 Palmerston Road 01-520 6051		0900-1730, ADC Wed
Riley, 246 Higham Hill Road 01-527 2045		0900-1800, ADC Th
Russell, 5 Chingford Road 01-527 4946		0900-1730, EDC Th
Wood Street Auto Parts,127 Wood Street 01-520 4050	0900-1800,	1000-1300 Sun
EC1 Angel, 395 St John Street 01-278 7793	0930-1800,	100-1600 Sat ECD Th
N5 Kirby, 69 Highbury Park 01-226 1508		0900-1730, ADC Mon & Th
N6 K & S, 389 Archway Road 01-340 6761		1000-1800 (1900 Fri)
N7 Pascall, 146a Seven Sisters Road 01-272 6302		0900-1730, ADC Th
N8 Day, 104 High Street 01-343 1644		0900-1700, ECD Th
Robert's Rebuilds, 2 Middle Mews 01-348 7621	1000-1800,	ADC Th, ECD Sat
N9 Jaggs, 2 Market Parade 01-807 5961		0900-1800, ADC Th
Recorder, 325 Fore Street 01-807 3719		0900-1730, ADC Th

N10 Hill Cycles, Fortis Green Road 01-883 4644   0930-1730, ADC Mon & Th
N11 Dare, 155 Bowes Road 01-888 2304   0900-1800. ECD Th
N12 Oscroft Bros, 191 Woodhouse Road 01-368 2914   0830-1800, EDC Wed
    Shorter Rochford, 65 Woodhouse Road 01-445 9182   1000-1800, ADC Th
N13 Hanlon, 77 Bowes Road 01-888 6607   0915-1800, ADC Th
N14 Arkay, 165 Bramley Road 01-363 9606   0900-1730, ECD Th
N16 Pascall, 143 Stoke Newington Road 01-254 3380   0900-1700, ECD Th
N18 Friendle, 111 Silver Street 01-807 1782   0900-1730, ECD Th
N22 Day, 570 Lordship Lane 01-888 2686   0900-1730, ECD Th
NW1 Chamberlaine, 75 Kentish Town Road 01-485 3983   0830-1800, ECD Th
    The Whizzer, 72 Crowndale Road 01-387 8813   1230-1800, ADC Mon & Sat
NW4 Dare, 4 Sutton Parade 01-203 4924   0930-1700, ADC Wed
    Hendon, 23 Bell Lane 01-203 2256   0900-1800 (1730 Th), 1000-1300 Sun)
NW5 Simpson, 116 Malden Road 01-485 1706   0900-1800, ADC Th
NW6 Beta Bikes, 275 West End Lane 01-794 4133   0900-1800, ADC Th
    Whisker, 80 Willesden Lane 01-624 6375   0900-1700, ADC Mon & Th
NW7 Bittacy Cycles, 18 Bittacy Hill 01-346 5784   0930-1800, ADC Wed,
    ECD Sat, 0900-1300 Sun
NW9 Bird, 273 Edgware Road 01-205 6035   0915-1730, ADC Th
    Clark, 509 Kingsbury Road 01-204 4165   0930-1730, ADC Mon
NW10 Fudge, 178 Church Road 01-459 7343   0900-1800, ADC Th
    Fudge, 30 Craven Park Road 01-965 5269   0900-1800
NW11 Car Parts, 752 Finchley Road 01-458 5716   0900-1800. ADC Th,
    1000-1300 Sun
SE1 Evans, 77 The Cut 01-928 4785   0930-1730 (1700 Sat), ADC Th
    Tandem Centre, 281 Old Kent Road 01-231 1641   0900-1800
SE5 Edwardes, 78 Camberwell Church Street 01-703 4077   0900-1700, ADC Th
    Edwardes, 221 Camberwell Road 01-703 3676   0900-1730, ADC Th
SE6 Compton, 25 Catford Hill 01-690 0141   0900-1800 (1700 Sat), ADC Th
SE8 Witcomb, 21 Tenners Hill 01-692 1734   0830-1730 (1630 Th)
SE9 Hili, 57 Well Hall Road 01-850 2446   0930-1730, ECD Th
    Lawson, 65 Avery Hill Road 01-850 5618   0930-1730, ADC Wed & Th
SE10 Young, 85 Trafalgar Road 01-858 7130   0930-1745 (1730 Sat), ADC Th
SE11 Edwardes, 240 Kennington Park Road 01-735 5176   0900-1730, ADC Th
SE13 Young, 290 Lee High Road 01-852 6680   0900-1745 (1730 Sat), ECD Th
SE15 Wilson, 32 Peckham High Street 01-639 1338   0930-1730
SE18 Blackett, 49 Woolwich New Road 01-854 6588   0930-1730, ADC Th
    Perry, 26 Woolwich New Road 01-854 2383   0930-1730, ADC Th
SE19 Bird, 37 Anerley Road 01-778 5330   0900-1730, ECD Wed
    Central, 7 Central Hill 01-670 1780   0900-1800, ADC Wed
SE20 Holdsworth, 55 High Street 01-778 7714   0900-1800 (1730 Sat), ADC Wed
SE23 Cooper, 49 Honor Oak Park 01-699 8711   1000-1900 Tu, Fri, Sat only
    Phoenix, 120 Stanstead Road 01-699 8309   0900-1800
SE25 Craggs, 211 Portland Road 01-654 2681   0900-1730, ADC Wed
SW1 Bicycle Revival, 17 Elizabeth Street 01-730 6716   0930-1830 (1730 Sat)
    Victoria Bicycle Co, 53 Pimlico Road 01-730 6898   0900-1800
SW4 Peter's, 118 Ferndale Road 01-274 5892   0930-1800
SW6 Patrick, 107 Lillie Road 01-385 9864   0900-1730. ECD Th
    Smallwood, 213 Dawes Road 01-385 3870   0900-1800, ECD Th
SW7 Rent-a-Bike, 3 Kendrick Mews 01-581 2044   1000-1800, ADC Sat
SW8 Lyons, 194 Wandsworth Road 01-622 3069   0900-1800, ADC Th
SW11 Saville, 97 Battersea Rise 01-288 4279   0900-1730, ADC Wed
SW15 Holdsworth, 132 Lower Richmond Road 01-788 1060   0930-1800, (1730 Th)
SW18 Algurns, 569 Garrett Lane 01-946 7921   0930-1800, ECD Wed
    Stratton, 101 East Hill 01-847 1381   0900-1800, ADC Wed

SW19 A W Cycles, 23 Abbey Park 01-542 2534   0900-1730, ECD Wed
Reed, 147 Kingston Road 01-542 4752   0900-1730 (1700 Sat), ADC Wed
Smith Bros., 14 Church Road, Wimbledon Village 01-946 2270
0900-1730, ADC Mon
Warner, 24 Colliers Wood High Street 01-540 4076   0900-1800, ECD Wed
SW20 Woolon, 57 Approach Road 01-542 4076   0900-1800, ADC Wed

W3 Rent-a-Bike, Student Centre, Kensington Church St. 01-937 6089
0930-1830 inclu. summer Sun
W4 Fudge, 176 Chiswick High Road 01-994 1485   0930-1800, ADC Th
Woolsey, 28 Acton Lane 01-994 6893   0900-1800, ECD Wed
W5 Ealing, 16 Bond Street 01-567 3557   0900-1730 (1700 Sat)
W9 Fudge, 564 Harrow Road 01-969 5991   0900-1800
W12 Fudge, 101 Uxbridge Road 01-743 5265   0900-1800
Nash, 155 Goldhawk Road 01-743 5133   0900-1800, ECD Th
Newton, 65 Askew Road 01-743 4422   0930-1730, ADC Th
W13 Denmar, 6 Leeland Terrace 01-567 7865   0900-1800 (1600 Sat), ADC Mon
W14 Bicycle Revival, 28 North End Parade 01-602 4499   0900-1800 (1730 Sat)
WC1 Condor, 144 Grays Inn Road 01-837 7641   0930-1800
WC2 Covent Garden, 41 Shorts Gardens 01-836 1752   1000-1800 (1700 Sat),
ECD Wed
Cycle Service Centre, 12 Flitcroft Street 01-379 7954   0900-1900 (1700 Th)
Barking Vickers, 39 London Road 01-594 2703   0900-1800
Barkingside Marments, 53 High Street 01-550 1633   0900-1730, ECD Th
Barnet Howard, 176 High Street 01-449 0784   0915-1730
Brentford Kay, 196 High Street 01-560 3836   0900-1730, ECD Th
Bromley Coopers, 646 Downham Way 01-857 4287   0900-1730 (1700 Sat), ADC Th
Hills, 481 Bromley Road 01-698 4197   0900-1730, ECD Th
Palmer, 19 Masons Hill 01-460 4456   0900-1700, ADC Wed
Burnt Oak Farrell, 14 Holmstall Parade 01-205 6693   0930-1800, ADC Th
Chadwell Heath Pask, 98 High Road 01-590 3322   0900-1800, ECD Th
Crayford Crayford, 191 Crayford Road (2) 521748 0930-1400, 1500-1730, ADC Wed
Croydon Allin, 57 Whitehorse Road 01-684 1620   0900-1800 (1730 Sat)
Butler, 9 South End 01-688 5094   0900-1800, ECD Wed
Dagenham Patco, 427 Becontree Avenue 01-590 1605   0900-1745, ADC Th
Shirley, 191 Broad Street 01-592 0468   0900-1730, ADC Th
Sissleys, 72 Moreton Parade 01-592 1824   0900-1730, ADC Th
Edgware Judd, 415 Burnt Oak Broadway 01-952 6911   0830-1730 (1655 Sat),
ADC Th
Enfield Bonners, Baker Street   1200-2000, ADC Wed
Broadway, 65 Windmill Hill 01-367 6690   0900-1700, ADC Wed
Carnaby, 114 St Marks Road 01-363 4091   0900-1800, ADC Wed
Halliday, 170 High Street 01-804 3462   0900-1730, ECD Th
Reliance, 210 Baker Street 01-363 8618   0900-1730 (1700 Sat)
Gant's Hill Grimstead, 137 Beehive Lane 01-550 0186   0930-1800
Harefield Clarke, 40 High Street (420) 2279   0900-1730, ADC Wed
Harold Hill Jeffrey, 106 Hilldene Avenue Ingrebrn (45) 43087 0900-1730, ADC Wed
Hayes Mal Rees, 13 Coldharbour Lane 01-573 2402 0930-1730 (1700 Sat), ADC Mon
McKellow, 1310 Uxbridge Road 01-573 3460   0900-1730, ADC Wed
Rowley, 50 Coldharbour Lane 01-573 1060   0900-1745, ADC Wed
Underhill, 988 Uxbridge Road 01-573 6857   0930-1715, ADC Wed
Hillingdon Holden, 16 Sutton Court Road Uxbridge (89) 35720   0900-1800,
ECD Wed
Hornchurch Dayberns, 3a Tadworth Parade (49) 51406   0900-1800, 1000-1300 Sun
Foster, 108 Ardleigh Green Road (49) 43728   0900-1730, ECD Wed
John's, 200 High Street (49) 41746   0900-1800, ADC Th

Kenley Kenley, 244 Godstone Road 01-660 8360 · 0900-1800, ADC Wed
New Malden Pitfield, 137 Kingston Road 01-949 4632 · 0830-1730, 0900-1700 Sat, ECD Wed
Northolt Viscount, 492 Church Road 01-845 6144 · 0930-1730, ADC Wed
Northwood, 118 Pinner Road (65) 24174 · 0830-1730, ADC Mon
Orpington Westdale, 2 Bridge Road (66) 39344 0900-1800 (1700 Sat), 1000-1400 Sun
Bird, 35 High Street, Green Street Green (66) 53746 · 0900-1730, ECD Th
Pinner Eastcote, 202 Field End Road 01-866 6876 · 0900-1730, ECD Wed
Rohan, 451 Rayners Lane 01-868 6262 · 0900-1800, ADC Wed
Richmond Richmond, 36 Hill Street 01-940 6961 · 1000 (0900 Sat)-1800 (2000 Th), 1100-1600 Sun, ADC Mon
Romford Crown, 183 London Road (70) 65370 · 0900-1730, ECD Th
John's, 162 Rush Green Road (70) 61047 · 0900-1800, ADC Wed
O'Brien Rory, 134 North Street (70) 41588 · 0900-1800 (0900 Fri, 1730 Sat), ADC Th
Ruislip Addy, 61 Swakeleys Road (71) 75376 · 0900-1730, ECD Wed
Fudge, 54 Victoria Road (71) 33576 · 0930-1800 (1900 Fri)
West End, 14a Newpond Parade (71) 38843 · 0930-1800 (1900 Fri)
Sidcup Argent, 11 Market Parade 01-300 5345 · 0900-1730, ADC Th
Potter, 136 Station Road 01-300 1328 · 1000-1800, ECD Th
Southall Cycle Centre, 122 The Broadway 01-574 1782 · 0900-1730, ADC Wed
Swan, 12 Norwood Road 01-574 5751 · 0900-1800, ADC Wed
Sutton Pearson, 126 High Street 01-642 2095 · 0900-1730, ECD Wed
Thornton Heath Boxall, 92 Beulah Road 01-653 3896 · 0900-1730, ADC Wed
Upminster Sixar, 304 St Mary's Lane (86) 50255 · 0830-1800 (2000 Th), ADC Wed
Wallington Ross, 6 Ross Parade 01-647 6121 · 0900-1800, ADC Wed
Wealdstone Bunting, 7 Masons Avenue 01-427 5136 · 0900-1800, ECD Wed
Welling Holdsworth, 69 Bellgrove Road 01-304 2832 · 0900-1800, ADC Wed
Wembley Sudbury, 771 Harrow Road 01-904 5966 · 0930-1730, ECD Wed
West Drayton West Drayton, 12 Station Road (81) 43530 · 0900-1725 (1700 Sat), ECD Wed
West Wickham Toplis, 17 Ravenswood Crescent 01-777 1084 · 0830-1715 (1730 Sat), ECD Wed
Whyteleafe Enquire Within, 244 Godstone Road Upr. Warlingham (820) 4059 · 1000-1800
Woodford Gunton, 720 Chigwell Road 01-504 1700 · 0900-1730, ECD Th

Essex
Chadwell St Mary Ray's, 101 Riverview (Tilbury 03752) 2601 0900-1730, ADC Wed
Grays Bersey, 26 Clarence Road (0375) 73777 · 0900-1730, ADC Wed
South Ockendon Tyson, 105 Daiglen Drive (700) 2181 · 0900-1730 (1700 Sat), ADC Wed

Hertfordshire
Borehamwood Denmar, 8 Leeming Road 01-953 3929 · 0915-1730, ADC Mon
Chesnut Hancock, 10 Cadmore Lane (Waltham Cross 97) 23922 · 0845-1745, ADC Th
Oxhey Thirteens, 73 Chalk Hill (Watford 92) 34221 · 0830-1730, ECD Wed
Rickmansworth Leisure Wheels, 153a Money Hill Parade (87) 74440 · 0930-1800 (1730 Sat), ECD Wed
St Albans Dean, 94 Victoria Street (56) 56509 · 0900-1800, ADC Th
Shenley Globe, 110 London Road (Radlett 779) 5830 · 0900-1800, ECD Wed
Waltham Cross Stanley Bridge, 186 High Street (97) 23012 · 0930-1730 (1800 Fri), ECD Th
Watford Haynes, 99 Longspring (92) 21706 · 0900-1730, ECD Wed
Neale, 26 Vicarage Road (92) 23916 · 0900-1715, ADC Wed
Woodford, 5 The Parade, Prestwick Road 01-428 3512 · 0900-1730, ADC Wed

Kent
Dartford O.T. 291 Lowfield Street (32) 25698   0900-1800, ECD Wed
   O.T., 79 East Hill (32) 74006   0830-1730
   Phillips, 78 High Street (32) 20435   0900-1730, ECD Wed
Gravesend Bridge, 18 Windmill Street (0474) 533748   0915-1800 ADC Wed

Chain store
Halfords stock a comprehensive range of cycle spares and undertake repairs.
There are branches in many High Streets.

APPENDIX F: ACCOMMODATION IN LONDON

As the city is visited by more tourists, including cycle-tourists, than any other in Britain, London has a wide variety of accommodation. High demand can, however, mean higher prices than in many other places.

Youth hostels

There are five hostels in London open to members of youth hostel associations. They are booked far in advance for most of the year.

City of London: 36 Carter Lane, EC4. 01-236 4965 (see map 1j).

Earl's Court: 38 Bolton Gardens, SW5. 01-373 7083. (see map 1h).

Hampstead Heath: 4 Wellgarth Road, NW11. 01-458 9054. (see map 3a).

Highgate: 84 Highgate West Hill, N6. 01-340 1831. (see map 3a).

Holland House: Holland Walk, W8 01-937 0748. (see map 1c).

The hostels at Epping Forest and Jordans are sufficiently near London for many cyclists and will often have more room. There are also hostels around London at Harlow, Ivinghoe, Lee Gate, Bradenham, Windsor, Tanners Hatch, Crockham Hill and Kemsing. Details can be found in the current YHA handbook.

Camping
There are three permanent camp sites in London:

Federation Road, Abbey Wood, SE2 01-854 8612.
Crystal Palace Parade, SE19. 01-778 7155.
High Road, Chigwell. 01-500 0121

There is also a campsite during the summer at Hackney Marshes, E5.

Bed & Breakfast, Hotels
Details of vacancies can be obtained from the London Tourist Board offices listed in Appendix C.

Establishments which particularly welcome cyclists are listed in the annual CTC handbook.

APPENDIX G BIBLIOGRAPHY

Cycletouring
The CTC Route Guide to Cycling in Great Britain and Ireland, Christa Gausden & Nicholas Crane: Oxford Illustrated Press, 1980.
Complements this book with 365 routes forming a byway network throughout Great Britain and Ireland. Complete with details of places of interest en route.

Adventure Cycling in Britain, Tim Hughes: Blandford, 1978.
A comprehensive cycle-touring text with advice on practicalities, technical information and a number of selected routes.

Basics
Know the Game — Cycling: EP Publishing in conjunction with the CTC. A good general guide to bicycles, riding and maintenance.

Skilful Cycling Royal Society for the Prevention of Accidents.
An inexpensive booklet on cycle control and safe riding techniques.

Maintenance
Richard's Bicycle Book, Richard Ballantine: Pan, 1979.
An excellent compedium of information and maintenance, well illustrated.

Cycling history
The Story of the Bicycle, John Woodforde: Routledge & Kegan Paul, 1970.
Traces the development of the bicycle from the hobby horse to the present day.

King of the Road, Andrew Ritchie: A well illustrated survey of cycling from its beginnings.

Physics
Bicycling Science, Frank Whitt & David Wilson: MIT Press, 1974.
A theoretical look at bicycle design and ergonomics. For the technically minded.

London
The Face of London, Harold Clunn: Hamlyn, 1970.
A comprehensive guide to London, including the suburbs.

The King's England, Arthur Mee: Two volumes: *The City and Westminster* and *North of the Thames except the City and Westminster.* Hodder and Stoughton, 1972.
A detailed guide to each of the London boroughs. Also other volumes covering the surrounding counties.

Blue Guide to London:
Red Guide to London:
Two books primarily aimed at the wealthy tourist, but containing some useful information. Little reference to outer London.

Buildings
Historic Houses, Castles and Gardens:
Museums and Galleries:
Two volumes published annually giving brief details and opening times of places throughout the British Isles.

Properties of the National Trust: with annual Properties Open supplement. Locations and useful descriptions of all National Trust properties in England and Wales.

Canals
Nicholson's Guides to the Waterways: Volume 1 South East: The official BWB guide to the canals with maps and notes on places en-route. Useful for towpath cycling.

Periodicals
Cycletouring:
The bi-monthly magazine of the Cyclists' Touring Club, covering touring, equipment and cycling developments in town and country. Free to CTC members but also available by subscription to CTC Headquarters.

Cycling:
A weekly cycling newspaper concentrating mainly on cycle racing but also some coverage of touring, equipment and general news.

Bicycle Times:
Cycling World:
Two monthly magazines dealing with touring and utilitarian cycling.

Time Out;
A weekly publication with details of events and entertainments in London.